WHICH REMINDS ME

○●○●○

WHICH REMINDS ME

○●○●○

by
Tony Randall
AND MICHAEL MINDLIN

The Delacorte Press Large-Print Collection

5227467

Published by
Delacorte Press
Bantam Doubleday Dell Publishing Group, Inc.
666 Fifth Avenue
New York, New York 10103

Library of Congress Cataloging in Publication Data

Randall, Tony.
    Which reminds me / by Tony Randall and Michael Mindlin.
        p. cm.
    ISBN 0-385-29785-8
    ISBN 0-385-29864-1 (Large-print ed.)
    1. Randall, Tony—Friends and associates.
2. Entertainers—
Anecdotes. I. Mindlin, Michael. II. Title.
PN2287.R245A3   1989
792'.028'092—dc20   89-11982
                                                                               CIP

Design and Illustrations by Jeremiah B. Lighter

Manufactured in the United States of America
Published simultaneously in Canada

November 1989

10   9   8   7   6   5   4   3   2   1

RRH

**This Large Print Book carries the
seal of approval of N.A.V.H.**

*To my mother and father, Betty and
Mike,
from whom I got a lot of love
and out of whom I got
my first laughs.*
M.M.
*To Mike and me
without whom this book would never
have been written.*
T.R.

Contents

The beginning

*T*HERE ARE, they tell me, more amusing anecdotes and jokes about show business than about any other. Cursed with almost total recall, I remember not only those in which I was personally involved but every one I have ever heard.

I decided to do something about putting them into a book on a dare from Mike Mindlin, an old friend, when we were swapping stories over lunch not too long ago in the Russian Tea Room. Mike has been around show business almost as long as I have, both here and abroad, as an advertising and publicity man in motion pictures, the theater, and ballet; a motion picture studio production executive; a documentarian, and a writer. We originally met in Maureen Stapleton's walk-up apartment on Manhattan's West Fifty-second Street when it was still a street of brownstones with little jazz clubs in their basements. It was known as Swing Alley. The developers hadn't come with their wrecking balls yet. Mike was dating Maureen at the time and she told me that every time she went out with him his mother sat shivah. (Sitting shivah is the Jewish ritual for mourning the dead.)

I remember the afternoon I met Mike especially well because of an odd little fellow—a silversmith, I was told—who sat listening quietly and laughing with a child's delight at the others—mostly actors—until Maureen said, "Wally, why don't you whistle some Bach for us?" "Oh, dear," he said, "we're going to do our tricks, are we?" and he started to whistle through his teeth, very loudly and with diabolical accuracy, one of the violin partitas, trills and all. Until then I thought I was the only one who could whistle a good trill and I showed him.

"You're whistling a fourth," he said. "A trill should be a second."

And then someone said, "Wally, do your Army sergeant," and he began, "Give me your attention, men . . ." and I slid down onto the floor in what my father used to call immoderate laughter.

And that was how I met Wally Cox, who was sharing an apartment in the Village with his childhood friend Marlon Brando.

Maureen's was always a great place to hang out. It was in 1947, we were all young and absolutely everything seemed possible.

I consider myself a fortunate man because I have always been paid so well for something I would gladly do for nothing. My profession is my hobby and recreation as well. Retirement for me, as it does for almost everyone in show business, will come involuntarily: when I die. And even then, I'm not so sure. As Neil Simon once put it, death is nothing more than nature's way of telling you to slow down.

I'm getting a little ahead of myself, but there is a story that expresses the show business attitude about death:

Two vaudevillians spent their entire professional lives together on tour, performing their act week after week, year after year, in theaters all around the world.

"Do you think there's a heaven?" one asked the other.

"Of course there is."

"But how can you be so certain?"

"Because I can't believe we could close here and not open someplace else."

A few of the stories you are about to read will, no doubt, seem familiar. That can't be helped. Mike once told our mutual friend, Larry Gelbart, a very gifted comedy writer *(Tootsie,* the TV show *M*A*S*H),* a rather famous Hollywood story that Larry had never heard. When Mike expressed his amazement, Larry said, "Mike, no one's heard them all."

—TONY RANDALL

○●○●○

The

actors

○●○●○

---○---

A friend said to an actor whose wife had died, "My heart bled for you at the church. I have never seen a man cry so much." "You should have caught me at the grave."

---○---

WHEN I WAS growing up in Tulsa, Oklahoma, I always knew that acting in the theater was what I wanted to do. It's still the thing I love to do most.

I tried Northwestern University for a year and then headed straight for New York, where I had always dreamed of being, and enrolled at the Neighborhood Playhouse, where Sanford Meisner taught me everything I know about acting.

I didn't work for the two years I was

studying my craft with Meisner. I was getting $10 a week from home and I could actually live on that. I remember there was a time when I needed some shirts and I asked my mother if she could send me an extra $10 so I could have three shirts made at Paul Stuart's. Made! Shoes at Thom McAn's were $2.50. There was an actor, Calvin Cantsen, who worked all the time but never earned more than Equity minimum, which in those days was $40 a week. When he died he left more than a couple of hundred thousand dollars to Actors Equity to buy shoes for actors who needed them. Actors wear out a lot of shoes making the rounds.

The life of an actor is extremely insecure. Over eighty percent of Actors Equity is unemployed. The profession requires complete dedication and devotion. The director Josh Logan once told an actor who was having some doubts about continuing in the career he had chosen, "If anything can stop you, let it."

Elliot Reed and Stanley Prager, two of my contemporaries, were struggling young actors who were barely surviving on their unemployment insurance. They went to a matinee of Fellini's *La Strada,* the Italian master's wonderful early film about an impoverished troupe of itinerant carnival performers and their travails.

"Oh," commented Prager after the picture ended, "what poor, pitiful people."

"Yes," responded Reed, "but at least they're working."

To illustrate just how insecure the life of a stage actor is, here is the first of what will undoubtedly be many apocryphal stories:

There is a rule in the legitimate theater that if an actor is not fired within the first five days of the rehearsal period, he cannot be replaced. His notice must be in writing and it must be delivered by the stage manager. This particular actor hid in the basement when he wasn't needed during the first five days—if they didn't see him they couldn't fire him. If only he could make it out of the theater the last day without anyone noticing. But just as he was opening the stage door, he heard the stage manager call out to him. His heart began to pound. The stage manager handed him a note. He read it and looked up with a great smile: "My mother died!"

Back in those very early days I used to play a lot of paddleball with Mason Adams, a fellow actor, and very often he'd say, "Gee, I've got to go to the dentist so we'll have to finish sooner," or "I can't play tomorrow. I've got to go to the dentist." I couldn't understand why anyone had to go to the dentist so often until I finally realized that dentist was the current euphemism in show business for psychoanalyst. Everyone, it seemed, when there was still some slight secret attached to the need for psychotherapy, was going to the "dentist."

Mr. Meisner had a student at the Neighborhood Playhouse who suffered from extraordinary stage fright, far beyond anything that was considered normal. (Peter Ustinov throws up in his dressing room before every performance, but he thought everyone did.) He'd break out in sweat, faint, have rapid, shallow breathing, and shake from head to foot. It made a life for him as an actor virtually impossible. At the end of his first year at the Playhouse he asked Meisner for help in finding work.

"Let's face it," Meisner said to the young man, "you're not ready. You need a dentist."

The first day of the fall semester the boy walked up to Meisner, opened his mouth in a huge smile and said, "Look!" The boy had spent his entire summer and a small fortune having all his teeth capped.

Meisner had us improvise a lot in our scenes, not out of any disrespect for the writer, but as a valuable tool to explore the possibilities of the scene. Another thing Meisner tried to teach us was that the character we were playing had a background—a history—that his life didn't begin when he walked out on the stage. It was up to each actor to create his character's biography—a back story—that brought him up to the point when he walked onstage.

Alan Dreeben, someone I grew up with in Tulsa, was so impressed with some of the things I told him about studying with Meisner that he stopped working as an actor and went to the Playhouse for a year. But one year really wasn't enough to grasp and assimilate it all, and so at times Alan would misapply certain techniques.

Alan and I went to audition for Robert Ross, a friend of Alan's, when we found out he was going to direct Laurence Olivier and Vivien Leigh in *Romeo and Juliet* on Broadway. We did the Brutus–Cassius scene from *Julius Caesar.* Alan began his speech, "Remember the Ides of March . . ." ending with "I had rather be a dog, and bay the moon,/ Than such a Roman." We were doing fine until Alan said, "I had rather be a dog, and bay the moon,/ Than such a Roman, for Christ's sake."

Alan had decided to improvise!

When I was in the Army, stationed in

Washington, Maurice Evans's famous production, the GI *Hamlet,* came through. Alan was in it—he was the Player King—and he and I went downtown after the show to have a bite together. Alan confided to me that Evans didn't like him. "Why not?" I asked.

"Well, while Evans is doing that speech—'Speak the speech, I pray you . . .'—I'm playing where have I seen Hamlet before?" Alan, as he had been taught by Meisner, had invented circumstances that existed before his entrance in the play. Through most of Hamlet's speech Alan's thinking, "Where do I know this guy from? Did we play this castle last year?" And then Alan told me he wanted to snap his fingers—as if to say, *I've got it! I remember!* "But," Alan told me forlornly, "Evans won't let me do it."

Among the invaluable things Meisner taught me about acting technique is that acting is exactly the same—there's no less, no more—whether it's for television, films, or theater. Acting is acting. You don't have to make it bigger for the stage or pull it down for the camera. Reality is reality wherever it is.

Alec Guinness, for one, feels exactly the same way about it: an actor must be most truthful and alive in whatever medium. When you see a great actor like Marlon Brando doing it—my God! When Marlon is alone in that room with his wife's corpse in that remarkable scene in *Last Tango in Paris,* his intensity is overwhelming. He's not pulling it down. He wouldn't have done it any differently in the theater.

Others, like Laurence Olivier, say you make it bigger onstage and hold it down in front of a camera. It doesn't become me to disagree with the great Lord Olivier, I know, but I do. I think that people who've seen him in movies only may sometimes wonder why he's called the world's greatest actor. Onstage, when he was at his best, he was absolutely a wild animal: he was terrifying—those incredible, remarkable explosions of energy. They were manic—electrifying. And I rarely saw that from him onscreen, where I think he should have been the same.

The war screwed up my generation completely. I was gone four years. Eli Wallach was gone six. When we came back from the Army we were no longer kids. We had to start all over again. All of us in my generation who "made it" did it the way Eli and I did—rather late in life. It didn't happen for me until 1952, when I did *Mr. Peepers* on television.

I got my very first job acting on Broadway after the war in Shakespeare's *Antony and Cleopatra* with the great Katharine Cornell. Unlike our British cousins, we actors in America don't get to do Shakespeare very frequently. For many years Shakespeare was actually performed far more often in the Yiddish theater by such gifted and colorful actors as Maurice Schwartz, Boris Thomashefsky, and Jacob Adler, than on Broadway. When Louis Calhern flew to New York from Los Angeles to star in Robert L. Joseph's production of *King Lear*, he got into a taxi at the airport for the trip into Manhattan. The Jewish cabbie recognized him.

"What are you doing in New York, Mr. Calhern?"

"I'm here to do *King Lear* on Broadway."

The driver scoffed. "It'll never go in English."

I played Scarus, a young Roman soldier, in that Cornell production. It was what we call a messenger part and they're always difficult if not impossible to play. "Of course it's difficult to play," the director almost always says, "that's why I got you." A character comes onstage and describes something very important that has happened offstage that the playwright for one reason or another was unable to show. In this case it is the entire battle of Actium, one of the great battles of history. And in six lines, this breathless young soldier must describe the slaughter of tens of thousands, the sinking of an entire fleet, and the fall of an empire. These parts usually go to actors who are relatively inexperienced.

○ 18 ○

It was a long show, and so "half-hour"—which is how long before the show starts actors are required to be in the theater—was at seven o'clock. I didn't go on until about ten o'clock but I spent three hours every night preparing intensely for my entrance. I banged my fists against the wall until they almost bled and shook the fire ladder backstage until it almost came off the wall, trying to experience the battle, trying to work myself into such a state of rage and frustration and despair that when I came onstage the audience would see the entire historic event. One night just as I was about to go on, Miss Cornell said to me, "Tony, some night why don't you try *not* preparing?"

So the next night I went on without preparing and gave exactly the same performance.

David O. Selznick, the legendary Hollywood producer, was in New York looking for a young actor to appear in one of his forthcoming films. He had seen the show, in which I wore a fine costume—a shield, a helmet, and sword—and made a fairly decent impression. He sent for me. You can imagine how excited I was. He was staying in a sumptuous suite at the Hampshire House. The living room seemed as big as a basketball court to me. I had to walk across it for what seemed an eternity to approach Selznick, who was seated all the way at the opposite end. It was, as we say in the theater, a difficult cross. As I approached him without the benefit of that beautiful costume and stage makeup, I could see his expression change. Just as I got to him and offered my hand, he said, "You're no dreamboat, Randall." John Derek got the part. Maybe it was good that I wasn't a dreamboat. This way, I had to learn to act. But for a while I was known along Broadway as "No Dreamboat" Randall.

I also did Shaw's *Caesar and Cleopatra* on Broadway with Lilli Palmer and Sir Cedric Hardwicke. Lilli and I got along very well but she was very temperamental. Closing night I came to her dressing room to say my good-byes and also to ask for a job. I knew that the following season she and her husband, Rex Harrison, were doing a play by John Van Druten—*Bell, Book and Candle*—and I had heard there was a very good part in it that I would be right for. I knew she liked my acting because once during rehearsals Sir Cedric, who was directing as well, decided to sit out front and watch the whole show. He asked me to play his part and so I walked through the whole play with the book in my hand reading Caesar. Lilli whispered to me, "I wish Cedric had some of your fire and humor." I knew just reading it that day that I was better than Cedric. He had no energy. He just barely dragged himself through it.

I knocked on Lilli's dressing-room door that last night and I couldn't hear whether the response was "Come in" or "Wait." I knocked again and she opened the door. She was livid. "What the hell are you doing?" "Oh, I'm sorry. I just came to say good-bye." "Good-bye," she said, and closed the door. A little later we were standing backstage waiting to make an entrance together and I said, "I'm sorry I

○ 21 ○

disturbed you earlier. I just wanted to say good-bye and mention *B.B.C.*" And she said, "Congratulations," which struck me as an odd response.

Some years later in London, Lilli was now married to Carlos Thompson and appearing on the West End with Noel Coward. I was by this time quite well known. She had a party after theater one evening —not a lot of people. Kim Novak and her then husband, Richard Johnson, a very handsome actor with the Royal Shakespeare Company, were there. I asked Lilli if she remembered that last night on Broadway. She had a dim memory of it. "I remember you told me something about going to work for the BBC." "No, no," I said, "I was asking you for a job in *Bell, Book and Candle*!" "Well," she said, "why didn't you come right out with it? You're much better than the guy we got."

The most common question laymen ask actors is how we remember our lines. Very often we don't. One of the things that all actors have in common is the fear of forgetting their lines during a performance. It has never happened to me except in a musical during a song—once in *Oh Captain!* the musical version of that wonderful Alec Guinness movie *Captain's Paradise,* and once on opening night of *The Music Man* when I was obsessed with getting through the terribly difficult lyric of "Trouble." I was so relieved when I made it that I relaxed into the next number, "76 Trombones," only a couple of minutes later. I completely forgot that there were "110 cornets" and sang "lots and lots of cornets." Otherwise, I'm one of the lucky ones. But "going up," which is the theatrical expression for it, is something that happens to all of us, and to the best of us and sometimes on opening night, as it did to me.

Herman Shumlin, who directed Ethel Barrymore in her biggest hit, *The Corn Is Green,* told me that on opening night Miss Barrymore went blank. It was in the middle of a scene when she was confiding a secret about another woman. She looked around furtively and said to the actor onstage with her, "Don't move." She then went offstage, got the line from the stage manager, came back stealthily, and said, "It's all right, she's not around," and proceeded with the line she had forgotten.

One of my first jobs in the theater was with Miss Barrymore in the Subway Circuit production of *The Corn Is Green.* In those days a hit show would extend its New York run by playing a month or so after it closed on Broadway in Brooklyn, The Bronx, Scarsdale, and Passaic. We played six nights and four matinees a week in midsummer in the days before air conditioning. It was grueling. Miss Barrymore was nearly seventy. In one scene she had to drag an unruly child up a steep flight of stairs and lock her in her room. There were some nights when she was just too tired and she'd say, "March yourself upstairs and lock yourself in your room."

During the opening night performance of Jean Anouilh's *Becket* on Broadway, Sir Laurence Olivier went up on his lines. Olivier whispered to the young

American actor who was onstage with him, "Give me my line." The actor just turned away.

Backstage afterward Olivier asked him why he had refused to give him his line. The young method actor said, "I don't work that way."

Guthrie McClintic, who directed *Winterset,* Maxwell Anderson's play about the Sacco and Vanzetti case, told me a horror story about that great play's opening night. McClintic wasn't an exceptionally good director but it didn't matter. He loved actors and the theater. He was stage-struck—more than anyone I've ever known. He was there at every performance unlike most directors, whom you never see again after opening night. Guthrie would sit backstage on the floor just listening to the play, often weeping, and in between the matinee and the evening performance he'd often go to sleep right there. Many actors gave their career-best performances for him simply because he loved them so much.

Winterset, which made a star of Burgess Meredith, was written—as all good plays really are—around one key speech. To make this one pivotal speech, McClintic wanted the finest actor he could get to play the old judge, the man who sentenced Sacco and Vanzetti to death and went through life thereafter tortured and tormented by the enormous miscarriage of justice he had committed. Driven half mad by his guilt, the judge became a derelict who lived under the Brooklyn Bridge.

The actor McClintic hired was Richard Bennett, the father of Constance and Joan, the Hollywood stars. A very great actor, the one Stanislavsky admired most when he came to America, Bennett fulfilled all of McClintic's expectations.

Opening night on Broadway, Maxwell Anderson and McClintic stood together in the back of the theater. It was a difficult play, in verse, and although the audience was respectful, it was impossible to tell if they liked it. Everything depended on the big moment in the third act when Bennett, as the Judge, huddled by the fire, made the speech. But it never came. Bennett blithely left out the entire speech!

Anderson and McClintic left the theater and walked down the street to a bar. All was over. All was lost.

The reviews the next day were all raves. Apparently the play did not need its key speech.

Going up and forgetting exactly where you are in a play is more apt to happen when it's late in a play's run and there are a lot of entrances and exits. It's very hard to keep them all straight, particularly when the play isn't guiding you. You're in the first act and all of a sudden you find yourself doing the end of the play.

Keenan Wynn once told me the most nightmarish theater story I've ever heard. He was the stage manager of the Boston company of *Room Service.* The actors always had to be letter perfect because they never knew when George Abbott, the director, was going to drop in on a performance. Wynn, as the stage manager, had to make certain that the actors stuck to every syllable. That's a very hard thing for a stage manager to do—to stay concentrated on the book for every performance and if there's a deviation of any sort to give the offending actor a note about it. *Room Service* ran so long that sometimes Wynn would drift off.

It got through to Keenan at one performance that the actors onstage were ad-libbing. He saw to his horror that Charles Dingle, who played the hotel manager, had not made his third-act entrance. Dingle had at least fifteen entrances in the farce and with each one, his character introduced still another plot complication. While the actors continued to improvise, Keenan ran around the back of the set to the other side of the stage to look for Dingle. Dingle wasn't there. Wynn then ran into Dingle's dressing room and there he was in his underwear, bending over the sink washing off his makeup. Dingle had come offstage at the end of the second act and forgotten that there was still another entire act. Keenan knew that if he yelled at him, "Charlie, you're on!" or some such words, the actor might have a heart attack. So very softly he said, "Charlie . . . Charlie. . . ." Dingle turned around and, as he wiped the water off his face, said, "What?" And then, without a word from Wynn, the awareness struck:

"Oh, no . . . oh, no . . . oh, no. . . ." Dingle said, hopping while trying to get back into his pants. "Oh, no, oh, no, oh, no. . . ."

Something not quite as extreme happened when I was appearing on Broadway in *Inherit the Wind,* when we had been running for a long time. The first big scene in the play is the picnic welcoming to town the character based on William Jennings Bryan, played by Ed Begley. Bryan, a rather pompous figure, thanks the church ladies and townspeople for their warm welcome. Paul Muni, the star of the play, had the greatest stage voice I have ever heard. Begley's was almost as powerful. At this particular performance, when Begley got to the line "I want to thank all the members of the Ladies' Aid for preparing this delightful picnic repast," he said instead, "I want to thank all the ladies of the Members' Aid . . . for belcome our foo." Begley just stood there looking as serious as ever as this absolute gibberish came out of his mouth. Someone had the presence to start the hymn singing—it was "Give Me That Old-Time Religion"—before all fifty actors onstage could break up.

When the trial ends in the play, the Scopes character is convicted, for he has, in fact, violated the Tennessee law against the teaching of evolution. Well into the second year of the play's Broadway run, as the Judge finished sentencing Scopes ("I find you guilty and fine you $100") all of us onstage—I played the H. L. Mencken character, Paul Muni was Clarence Darrow—and in the audience clearly heard Begley say in an absolutely normal voice, "Oh, that cunt!" Logic told me and everyone else that we could not have heard William Jennings Bryan say what we had all just heard him say! We blocked it out. So did the audience. It was as if it had never happened.

○ 30 ○

Whenever I walk past what was once one of Broadway's most beautiful little theaters, the Henry Miller on West Forty-third Street, which has, of late, been subjected to a succession of desecrations, I think of the great actor Henry Miller, who built it. Late in his career Miller found it increasingly difficult to remember his lines. His stage manager suggested that he always keep his "sides" in his pocket. (Sides are half pages on which there are only your character's lines and the cues leading into them. With the advent of copying machines we don't use them anymore.) Both Miller and the actress he was appearing with onstage went up on their lines. Miller very calmly removed the sides from his pocket, walked downstage, unembarrassed, to the footlights so he could see better, found his place while everyone in the audience and onstage waited, and said, "Well, it's not me."

Alfred Lunt and Lynn Fontanne were onstage with four other actors, well into the second year of one of their many long-running hits, when they all went up on their lines. The alert stage manager fed them the line from the wings but nothing happened onstage. The stage manager prompted them again and once more there was nothing but silence onstage. When the stage manager gave them the line a third time, Lunt whispered to him, "Yes, but who says it?"

There are actors like the famed matinee idol Otis Skinner, who were enormously quick witted and could ad-lib their way out of any predicament. When I was about fifteen and he was past eighty, I heard him lecture in Tulsa. He reminisced about nineteenth-century theater and did an imitation of Edwin Booth. Skinner once appeared on Broadway in a play in which the action called for him to shoot another character. However, the all-important prop, the gun, was nowhere in sight. Unfazed, Skinner walked across the stage, kicked the actor in the ass, turned to the audience, and said, "Luckily, the toe of me boot had poison in it!"

Celia Adler, of the renowned acting family known as the Yiddish Barrymores, was, from all I've ever been told, no less quick witted than Skinner. She was acting in a play in which she discovers during the course of a very high tea that the other character in the scene is having an affair with her husband. Adler reaches into a drawer, takes out a revolver, and shoots the other woman dead. Only at this performance, of course, when she opened the drawer there was no revolver in it.

Without hesitating any longer than Otis Skinner did, Adler scooped out all of the strawberry jam that was in the silver bowl on the tea tray, flung the blood-colored substance into the face of the other actress, and said, "Die!"

In the original production of Hecht and MacArthur's *Front Page*, that superb actor Osgood Perkins, Tony's father, was playing Walter Burns, the fast-talking newspaperman. He saw to his horror that the actor appearing as the escaped convict who is hiding in the rolltop desk at the end of the second act, was standing in the wings as the third-act curtain rose. There was panic. Nothing from that point on in the play works unless that character is hiding in the desk and his presence is revealed during the final act. Perkins collected himself in a matter of seconds and motioned with his eyes to the wayward actor to come around to the door of the set. Perkins opened the door and yanked the actor through it. As he pushed him inside the desk and rolled the top down he said, "And don't ask to go again!"

At times actors can get carried away in these situations. Frank Craven, whose performance as the Stage Manager in the original production of Thornton Wilder's *Our Town* is one I shall always remember, went up on his lines in *Village Green*. Craven, who was also a gifted playwright, began to ad-lib. His fellow actors onstage, Norman Lloyd and Matt Briggs, listened in awe at his virtuosic improvisational skills. After a while Briggs, concerned that Craven might fail to give him his cue, interrupted.

"Wait a minute! Wait a minute!" said Craven, who was on an improvisational roll. "Let me finish!"

○ 34 ○

I was at a performance of a play, *A Far Country,* about Freud, who was played by Steve Hill. Ludwig Donath, a lovely actor, played Breuer, Freud's mentor. Breuer was describing his first experiments with hypnosis which resulted in a kind of psychoanalysis in which a patient began to talk about his past and opened up the whole world to the possibilities of the subconscious.

"Believe me, my dear Freud," said Donath, who spoke with a middle-European accent, "it was the most exciting moment of my entire professional career. It was like opening a human skull and looking at the human brain with a microphone. Never in my entire life—in fifty years of practice, a practice which has taken me to many lands and the treatment of thousands of patients—*microscope*—have I had such an experience."

G. P. Huntley, an English actor who was a notorious drinker, was repeatedly warned by everyone that he would go up on his lines. He was doing Shakespeare in London when the inevitable happened: he went completely blank. The Bard's poetry is nothing anyone can ad-lib and so Huntley, in despair, sat down and buried his head in his hands. At that very moment the curtain came down and an announcement was made over the loudspeaker system: "Ladies and gentlemen, we regret to inform you that King George V has died."

The most unlikely prompt in the entire English-speaking theater? ". . . or not to be."

After a performance there are the inevitable backstage visitors, most of whom are very welcome, and some of whom are not.
    The best compliment I have ever been given—or for an all-too-brief moment it seemed to be—was backstage when I was a young actor on Broadway in 1954 in *Oh, Men! Oh, Women!* with Franchot Tone and Betsy Von Furstenberg. I had replaced Gig Young. One night, as I was taking off my makeup, a woman of middle years came into my dressing room with a doddering old man

who was so old that his ears flapped when he walked.

"Mr. Randall," he said, "my name is Edgar McGregor."

I was impressed. He had once been a very well-known Broadway director.

"I've been to see you in this play four times and you're the best I've seen since Willie Collier."

I was thunderstruck.

"I don't know what to say, sir. I've always heard he was the finest we've ever had in light comedy."

"That's right, he was."

"I know that John Barrymore said that everything he knew about acting he had learned from Willie Collier."

"That's right."

"Barrymore toured Australia with Collier in *The Boys of Company B* in 1906."

"That's right," said McGregor. "Were you with them?"

Herbert Marshall, the late English movie star who had lost a leg in World War I, came backstage after a performance to see Mike Nichols, then an actor. The doorman shouted up the stairs to Nichols, who was removing his makeup in his third-floor dressing room.

"Mr. Nichols, Herbert Marshall is here to see you."

Shouting back, Nichols said "Have him come up . . . er . . . I'll be right down!"

Estelle Winwood, the English actress best remembered for her role as Henry Higgins's mother in *My Fair Lady,* had a close friend who was understudying the lead in a Broadway play. She never got the opportunity to go on until one matinee when the star called in sick. Could Winwood possibly come to see her? "Of course."

That afternoon Winwood watched her friend give an atrocious performance. Knowing that she was expected backstage after the final curtain, Winwood grew increasingly anxious about what she was going to say. "I've never seen anything like it," or "Well, you've done it again," or any of the other noncommittal, evasive bromides all of us in the theater have used in a pinch would do.

The inspiration came to Winwood as she was embracing her friend in the dressing room.

"My darling," she said, "if only you could have been out front with me. . . ."

I dressed with Ed Begley in *Inherit the Wind.* One night after the final curtain as we trudged up the stairs, hot and exhausted, we saw that our dressing-room door was open. Inside we saw a well-dressed middle-aged couple who had seen the show, had somehow gotten past the stage doorman, and found our dressing room while we were taking our bows. They told us they were from Newport News, Virginia. Ed wore a big wad of padding on his stomach for his part. We couldn't undress because they wouldn't leave. They just stood there looking at us. The woman fixed her hair in our mirror. Silence. Ed said he'd once made a movie in Newport News. "Yes," the man said, "I remember. Say, here's a funny one: Gary Cooper was in that movie and we've got some friends named Cooper. That's the truth." I began to giggle hysterically. Ed began to moan. We all looked at him. He moaned some more and swooned to the floor. "Oh," said I, "he's having one of his seizures. I know what to do. You'd better let me handle this." And I got them out of there. But Ed had actually passed out from the heat. We never did find out who they were.

Burl Ives told me that some women in the audience were so strongly affected by the frank carnality of his part as Big Daddy in *Cat on a Hot Tin Roof* that many times during the run he'd find some woman waiting in his dressing room in high expectancy. That happened to me only once. It was between the acts of *Odd Couple.* I explained that I needed the full intermission to make a wardrobe and makeup change. The woman was deeply offended. "If I had known that I'd have gone to Jack Klugman's dressing room."

Oh, Men! Oh, Women! was a play about psychiatry. The entire first act of the play takes place in a psychoanalyst's office and most of the act is taken up with the sessions of two patients, each of whom has a long monologue. The audiences early in the run were fantastic: they roared with recognition at every line, every gesture. They were all the analysands in New York. But after this pool ran dry, the audiences didn't laugh as much. Late in the run a friend whose sexual inclinations were the subject of much speculation between my wife and myself—"Is he or isn't he?"—came backstage after a performance. But that night, when we saw the friend he'd brought with him, all doubt was silenced. We all went to the Blue Ribbon, a theatrical hangout, after the show. This man hated the women's clothes in the play. That's all he talked about. "Why did she wear pink in that scene, for God's sake? She looked like a strawberry ice cream soda." And in between comments like that he waved to celebrities seated around the restaurant. When he'd finished talking about all the women's clothes and the furniture and the drapes he said, "Of course this play means much more to me than it would to an ordinary playgoer."

"Why?" I asked.

"Because I'm a psychiatrist."

After all these years a Broadway opening, always so pregnant with wonderful possibilities, is still a thrilling occasion for me. In bygone days, during the theatrical season, which traditionally ran from September through May, as many as five or six plays opened—and often closed—every week. In the twenties, when as many as a couple of hundred musicals and straight plays opened during a season, sometimes two and three on the same night, newspapers had first-, second-, and third-string critics to keep up with all of the activity. Unfortunately there aren't nearly as many openings now as there once were—perhaps twenty-two in an average season—and, of course, in fewer theaters. The real-estate interests, far more powerful than I and others who have tried diligently to save theaters, have demolished more than a few. It makes me very sad and angry.

Well-wishing opening-night telegrams were once an art form. One of the wittiest was the one sent by Noel Coward to his lifelong friend Gertrude Lawrence when she opened in *Skylark,* her first appearance on Broadway in a nonmusical.

LEGITIMATE AT LAST, WON'T MUMMY BE PLEASED.

During the intermission of a celebrity-studded Broadway opening, Michael Wager, an actor, was pouring his heart out to a few close friends, tearfully telling them his tale of personal woe. His wife, it seems, had gone to Paris to visit her best friend, Ellen Adler, who was having an affair with René Liebowitz, a French classical musician. Wager's wife had then fallen in love and displaced Ellen in the musician's affections and had just informed Michael that she was remaining in Paris with her lover.

"I don't know what I'm going to do,"

the heartbroken actor went on. "She's abandoned me and our little daughter. This is the most dreadful thing that has ever happened to me. I—"

And then quite suddenly Wager interrupted himself.

"—Oh, look," he said, pointing across the crowded theater lobby, "there's Thornton Wilder!"

Milton Berle, very rarely at a loss for words, was at a Broadway opening and wanted to sneak away at the end of the atrocious first act. Just as he claimed his overcoat and hat from the cloakroom, the play's producer spotted him. What might have been an embarrassing moment Berle deftly turned around.

"God, it's so cold in there!" said Berle as he headed back into the theater.

And after the opening night come the reviews. In the good old days, not so long ago, when New York had seven newspapers, we would go to Sardi's after an opening and wait for the early editions.

In reviewing a play for *The New York*

Times, the acerbic George S. Kaufman called Sidney Blackmer "the worst actor in the world." Blackmer sued Kaufman and the *Times* and won. When Blackmer appeared next on Broadway, Kaufman was more cautious. His review didn't get to Blackmer until the very last sentence. "As for Sidney Blackmer," Kaufman wrote, "he wasn't up to his usual standards."

I am convinced that even the worst actor has one good performance in him if he's lucky enough to get the right part. Every actor has one part that he can play better than anybody else and that role for Blackmer was in *Come Back, Little Sheba.*

I shall always remember the review of *Streetcar* by Wolcott Gibbs of *The New Yorker.* He devoted exactly one sentence to Marlon Brando, who gave one of the most remarkable performances of this century!

I sometimes muse about what it would be like if people in other professions—most notably architects—had to go through the equivalent of an opening night. For example, 666 Fifth Avenue—so ugly that it's been described as the box the Seagram Building came in—is completed and opens. Paul Goldberger, the architecture critic of *The New York Times,* reviews the building and roasts it. The Tishmans, who own the building, close it and tear it down. If this were only so, perhaps architects would be a little more creative. We, after all, have to live with their mistakes for so long. Maybe they'd start opening their buildings out of town. 666 FIFTH AVENUE OPENS IN BOSTON, the banner headline screams, and the subhead reads, BUILDING CLOSES IN TWO DAYS.

Second to none in vitriol, the English theater critic Kenneth Tynan, who stammered, was a guest on David Susskind's television show. Tynan was asked which theater he preferred—the English or American.

"The American," Tynan replied.

"Why is that?" asked Susskind, who was somewhat surprised by his answer.

"B-b-because, the English theater re-re-reminds me of a g-glorious p-p-pool t-table: great l-legs, a b-b-beautiful green f-felt t-top and n-n-no b-balls!"

Tues. October 21
    Dear Diary,
    This is my final day in the salt mines. Tomorrow I will be a star. I've worked, I've paid my dues. I deserve it. I finally got the part of a lifetime. We open tonight on Broadway and tomorrow all my worries will be over. I've got the best scene that any actor in the history of the theater has ever had. It's all mine: I'm alone onstage for twenty minutes except for an actor playing an old man who sits upstage writing a letter. When that curtain comes down tonight, everything I have ever wanted in life is going to come true.

Wednesday, October 22
    He drank the ink.

○●○●○

All

those

others

○●○●○

---○---

Said George Cukor, the director, to Ruth Gordon, who was probably the most eccentric of all our great actresses, "Dear, you were born peculiar, you don't have to act peculiar."

---○---

ND THEN THERE are all those others —the directors, playwrights, producers, songwriters, lyricists—all those creatures who we actors tend to think were put here on earth for no other reason than to provide us with work. No less a theatrical eminence than George Bernard Shaw, in his essay "The Play of Ideas," seems to substantiate this generally held actors' view of themselves. The playwright's primary function, according to Shaw, is to invent for us—tragedians and clowns alike—stories and plots. Samuel Beckett, on the other hand, thinks, "The best possible play is one in which there are no actors, only the text."

The writers—playwrights, composers, lyricists—the true creators, not the interpreters—the ones who make everything possible, after all—are going to join their motion-picture and television brethren in a subsequent chapter of their own. The others I will deal with here, as best I can.

The theater has been and always will be the most precarious of all pursuits. Movies and television are what all of us do for money and the theater is what we do for love. Everyone in the theater has his ups and downs. The odds against any play or musical becoming a Broadway hit are daunting.

Herman Shumlin, the stage director I was closest to, was an amazing man, to whom the fates weren't at all kind. He had many hits on Broadway over the years but he had long stretches without any, especially toward the end of his career. *Inherit the Wind,* in fact, was his last hit and it was a huge one.

Our first, indirect connection came through *The Corn Is Green,* which he produced and directed on Broadway. After the show had been running for some time, Kermit Bloomgarden, Shumlin's general manager for years, hired me to understudy the lead and play a small part. But I didn't get to meet Shumlin until my then agent, Bill Liebling, took me to read for *Inherit the Wind.*

Shumlin had a reputation for being an exceedingly difficult man. Lillian Hellman barely mentions him in any of her books, and yet Shumlin directed and produced most of her important plays. As I came to know him, I realized he must have had a lot to do with the shaping of Hellman's works—that was his real strength. He would always work with the writers. But Hellman says so little about him that the silence is revelatory.

I read for Shumlin in his office. By then I was doing *Mr. Peepers,* which had become a successful television show, and

I was fairly well known. When I finished reading, Shumlin said to me, "Why is a man of your ability wasting his talent on television?" I stood up and screamed at him—as loudly as I have ever screamed at anyone in my life—"How dare you say that to me? How dare you? Ten years ago I stood on a line of actors two stories long waiting to get into your office to read for you and you wouldn't even see me! How dare you say that to me now?"

Shumlin stood up and screamed at me, "Don't blame me for your life! It's your life. You have no one but yourself to blame for it!"

And at that moment we became blood brothers. We almost fell into each other's arms. We had passed through every stage of acquaintanceship and friendship, falling out and falling back in again. The outer office was filled with other actors and they heard the two of us screaming at each other. The stories that went around Broadway and that came back to me—some of them years later in the most distorted forms—were unbelievable: that

Shumlin had attacked me physically; that I had attacked him and that we were rolling on the floor of his office and that I had picked up a lamp and hit him on the head and that he ordered me out of his office.

Shumlin and I became much more than just a director and an actor. From that instant we were like old friends. He was old enough to be my father but I could always talk to him as though I were the older man. It became one of those peculiar father-and-son relationships where the roles were reversed.

Not too long after *Inherit the Wind* opened on Broadway, Paul Muni suddenly came down with an eye tumor. He went right from the doctor's office to the hospital and his understudy, Sy Oakland, went on that night. Shumlin quickly wrote a speech which he had Ed Begley go out in front of the curtain to deliver. "Ladies and gentlemen, Mr. Muni has been stricken. However, no play is merely one actor. There are fifty-five fine actors in this cast and tonight the part of Henry Drummond will be played by that fine young actor Mr.

Simon Oakland." The entire audience got up and asked for their money back. Shumlin closed the show, we rehearsed with Melvyn Douglas for a couple of weeks and reopened.

After a few months Douglas called in sick one night with total laryngitis. Herman was able to find Sy Oakland, who had left the cast and was rehearsing with the Lunts in *The Great Sebastians*. Herman had learned his lesson. Instead of sending Ed Begley out he wrote a speech for me to deliver. "Guess what, folks? Sy Oakland's back. Are we in luck! He's left the Lunts and he's here with us tonight." Just before I went out, we discovered that the entire center section of the orchestra was filled with three hundred people who had come in on a special show train from Columbus, Ohio, led by the city's mayor and the governor of the state, later senator, Frank J. Lausche. Shumlin told me that immediately after I made the announcement about Sy I should introduce them. A spotlight found them and while the audience was applauding, Herman brought the curtain up. No one had time to ask for his money back.

The next performance Melvyn was still sick and Shumlin told me to go out and make the same announcement. I said, "Fine, Herman, but what saved us was the group from Ohio and the mayor and the governor." "Introduce them again." I said, "Herman, I can't do that." And he said, "I don't care. Introduce them again." And so I did. A spotlight moved all over the center section of the orchestra, the audience applauded, and once again the curtain went up before anyone had a chance to ask for a refund. Douglas missed another performance and Herman said, "Tony, the mayor and the governor have loved the show so much they've come back again tonight." I said, "Herman, I won't do it." "You do it or I'll have you up on charges at your union." "For what?" "Disobeying your director." So I went out and introduced them for a third time and Herman gave me a beautiful sweater.

There was an actor in *Inherit the Wind* who was timid, self-effacing, and nonassertive. You have to wonder why such people go onstage, but they do. Perhaps they think the stage will be their therapy. One of his lines was "This is the first time that such and such has happened." And from the first rehearsal on he'd say, "This is probably the first time that such and such has happened." At every rehearsal Herman would stop him and say, "No, no, it's not *probably,* it *is* the first time. That's the point of the line and that's why you must say it the way it's written." But the actor simply could not bring himself to be that definite—that specific. It was too contrary to his nature. At the end of the rehearsal on the day we opened on Broadway, Shumlin had notes for just about everybody in the huge cast of fifty-five actors. When he got to this actor he called his name—let's say it was Smith. No response. "Smith," Herman said again. Smith finally looked up and Herman said, "Do you remember me, Smith?" Opening night, "probably" was back in.

As Herman Shumlin grew old, everyone forgot his many hits and substantial contributions to the theater. (His first hit had been *The Last Mile.* The Broadway production made Spencer Tracy a star and the road company did the same for Clark Gable.)

People have short memories, even theatrical people. Newspapers too. I was in Los Angeles when Herman died and read his obituary in the *L.A. Times:* "Henry Shulman, Broadway producer . . ."

Tyrone Guthrie is another director I admired enormously, so much so that when I read he was starting a repertory theater in Minneapolis–St. Paul I wanted to go with him. My wife was against it. "There's snow on the ground nine months a year there." I thought Guthrie was the greatest director of the twentieth century. His *Troilus and Cressida, H.M.S. Pinafore,* and the grand operas he directed at the Met were all superb. The range of the man!

As much as I admired him, when I was offered a part in *The Tenth Man,* which he was signed to direct on Broadway, I turned it down. It just shows you what kind of theatrical acumen I have! I thought that if they didn't get a Jewish director for this—Herman Shumlin, Harold Clurman, Garson Kanin—they were crazy. They needed, I thought, someone who understands the Yiddishkeit of this play, this culture—someone who understands the people and the language. I was convinced Paddy Chayefsky was going to ruin his play if he gave it to this Englishman— Irishman, actually. Guthrie would turn it into a dazzling circus but it wouldn't be *The Tenth Man.* Well, it's as wrong as I've ever been in my life. Guthrie knew about Yiddishkeit. Don't ask me how. He was a genius. I guess he walked one day around the Lower East Side and absorbed it all through those extra pores he had in that six-foot-four-inch frame of his. He even did an *Oedipus Rex* in Hebrew, no less, with Israel's Habimah Theater.

After I read about his plans for the repertory theater, I tried calling him at his hotel in Manhattan, but he never returned my calls. I wrote to him half a dozen times and he never answered my letters. He was in rehearsals for *Gideon,* another Chayefsky play, and so I called Paddy and asked him to introduce me. Paddy told me to come by the theater on Thursday during a break in rehearsal. When I went, it was Yom Kippur and Paddy was in shul. So I hung around the stage door until this tall man came out. I introduced myself. "Oh, yes, Paddy's told me about you." He permitted me to take him to lunch and he drank two martinis. I told him how much I wanted to be with him in Minneapolis. "Oh, then, you're aboard. Now make a list of the twenty parts you'd like to play."

I made the list and sent it to him after *Gideon* opened. It included the greatest parts ever written for light comedians: Cyrano, Benedick, Hamlet. Light comedians have done well with *Hamlet*—Olivier, Gielgud, Barrymore. It's a part for a light comedian with a lot of emotion.

Six months passed and I was working on a picture in Rome, where a letter was forwarded from Guthrie turning me down. *"You do understand, old boy."* I was very disappointed. Angry too. I went out and bought a picture of the pope, scrawled *You lying bastard* across it, and mailed it to him. And would you believe it, he never had the courtesy to answer me! I saw him at the Dorchester in London some time after that. I smiled and he walked right by me. But he was so tall that perhaps he never noticed me.

Directors, at times, have been known to say terrible things to and about actors, who are, of course, overly sensitive. Alfred Lunt was directing Audrey Hepburn and her then husband, Mel Ferrer, in the Broadway production of *Ondine,* Jean Giraudoux's play about a knight who falls in love with a water nymph. Frustrated during a rehearsal because he wasn't getting what he wanted from Ferrer, Lunt threw his hands up in despair and exclaimed, "How can I make a knight errant out of a horse's ass?"

Josh Logan, one of Broadway's most successful directors, said in utter exasperation to Geraldine Page, one of the stage's most gifted but fidgety actresses: "For God's sake, just don't do something—stand there!"

I met Logan, some years ago, in a rather unusual way. I lived on the floor above Burton Lane, the great musical-comedy composer *(Finian's Rainbow, On a Clear Day)*. For one entire summer the building's back elevator was being repaired and so every night at eight the front doorbell would ring and you handed your garbage to one of the porters. One night when I was wearing jeans, no shirt, and no shoes—believe it or not, I'm a real slob around the house!—the front doorbell rang at eight. I ran into the kitchen, picked up the garbage, brought it to the front door, and thrust it into the hands of Josh Logan, who was standing there in his tuxedo next to his wife, Nedda. And he took it! The Logans were going to a party at the Lanes but had gotten off at the wrong floor.

Josh and I had seen each other from

time to time before then at my gym but never met. Josh never worked out but he took steambaths. He told me that he was in the steam room once, stark naked, sitting next to a very fat man with an extremely hairy body.

"Hey," the man said, putting his face right next to Logan's, "you're Josh Logan, aren't you?"

"Yes."

Without further ado the man stood right up and burst into "One Alone" from Sigmund Romberg's *Desert Song*. This business being what it is, you seize your opportunities whenever they present themselves.

George Abbott is probably the director with the most knowledge about comedy. At that two-martini lunch Guthrie called him "the old master." At this writing Abbott is over a hundred, newly married and still working. An actor in a show that had already opened on Broadway told Abbott that he was no longer getting the laugh that always came when he dialed a telephone. Abbott ducked into the theater to see him do the scene.

"You're dialing the wrong number."

"The wrong number?"

"Yes. You should be dialing ones, twos, and threes. You're dialing eights, nines, and zeros and it's taking much too long."

And sure enough, at the next performance the actor got his laugh back.

Kermit Bloomgarden, who became a very successful Broadway producer (*The Music Man, Death of a Salesman,* etc.), always had a terrible time remembering names. While talking to Reginald Rose, the award-winning writer of *Twelve Angry Men,* Bloomgarden said, "But that's exactly what, er—you know—er, what's his name—oh, God—a long time ago—he was so famous."

The name simply wouldn't come to him.

"Oh, you know who I mean," Bloomgarden finally said, thrusting both his arms straight out and tilting his head to one side:

When Howard Lindsay, who wrote many shows and was the coauthor and star of *Life with Father,* was dying, I visited him several times. He and his wife, Dorothy Stickney, a very successful actress who played his wife in *Life with Father,* stayed up most of the night looking at old movies on television. And they always played a game—who could recall the most names of the old-time actors. "Oh, there's Berton Churchill," "There's George Barbier," "Lionel Belmore"—almost all of them character actors who had died. One night, Dorothy told me, they were watching a real oldie with Henry Fonda and Dorothy couldn't figure out who the actress was who was playing Fonda's mother. "Who is that woman? Oh, we know her. She's so familiar. Who is it? Oh, my God! It's me!"

Peter Stone, the librettist of such Broadway shows as *1776, Woman of the Year,* and *My One and Only,* has a theory he once shared with me that the human brain has a maximum capacity of twenty-five thousand names. Once it's reached that limit, for every new name it takes in, an old one drops out. He no longer looks at the end credits of movies and television shows. He's afraid he'll forget his wife's name.

Billing is supremely important to almost everyone in show business. I say almost because it isn't to me. I have no ego about billing. How large and in what position my name appears relative to others in the *Playbill,* paid advertising, and so on, is far less important to me than salary. Frequently management offers you a choice —less money but bigger billing. There are some who find the blandishments of billing irresistible. I suppose they think it means status, and actors and directors and their agents, and for that matter everyone in the theater, are often zealous about it.

I can't imagine why, but a producer once tried to prevail on Alfred Lunt to give his wife, Lynn Fontanne, first billing.

"Fontanne and Lunt? This is the theater, dear boy," Lunt said, "not a goddamned lifeboat."

The great Italian actress Anna Magnani was late on the set one day during the filming of *The Fugitive Kind.*

"Where is she?" the director, Sidney Lumet, asked his assistant director.

"She's in her dressing room crying."

Lumet went to the star's dressing room and found her seated at her dressing table, tears pouring down her cheeks. Her costar, Marlon Brando, was sitting on the floor in a corner of the room.

"What's wrong, Anna?" Lumet asked.

"He," she cried out, pointing to

Brando, "won't even give me first billing in Italy!"

Some shows have come perilously close to falling apart when billing disputes have defied solution. Sometimes the Solomonian solution is to do it alphabetically. Jack Klugman and I were once actually introduced at a charity affair in the following way: "And now here in alphabetical order are Jack Klugman and Tony Randall!"

A brouhaha over billing very nearly shut down the Broadway musical comedy *Gypsy* while it was still aborning. In the lore of the theater it's come to be known as the Battle of the Boxes.

When the supremely gifted Jerome Robbins choreographed and directed *West Side Story,* he had the following billing in all the ads, posters, and programs:

> Entire Production
> Directed and Choreographed
> by
> JEROME ROBBINS

The box around Jerry's credit had always been a sticking point with Arthur Laurents, who wrote the libretto of *West Side Story*, as well as *Gypsy*. When Robbins was signed by David Merrick and Leland Hayward to direct and choreograph *Gypsy*, it was with the contractual agreement, at Laurents's insistence, that he would not have the box.

All was going smoothly until the Sunday *New York Times* ran a full-page ad for *Redhead*, a musical starring Gwen Verdon. The director and choreographer of the show, Bob Fosse, a former Robbins assistant, had a box around his name. Robbins now insisted, the contract notwithstanding, that he, too, must have a box around his name. Laurents, in response, was taking the position that if Merrick and Hayward, *Gypsy*'s coproducers, gave in to Robbins's demands, Laurents would invoke the rights he had under the provisions of the Dramatists' Guild and close the show.

Gypsy was not even in rehearsal yet and already its future was threatened. The dispute was finally resolved by giving Robbins his box and increasing Laurents's share of the box-office receipts.

Merrick's problems with Robbins were not limited to billing. At the end of a day during the rehearsal period, he was in his office with Mike Mindlin, who was his production associate at the time, angry and upset about another matter related to Robbins. Joe Kipness walked in. "Kippy," a Broadway producer and restaurateur, was quite an original character, powerful physically and tough, but genuinely warm and affectionate. He had all kinds of connections and would do just about anything for a friend.

"What's the matter, fellas?"

Merrick told him. What followed was the most generous and spontaneous offer I have ever heard of.

"Do you want me to have his legs broken?"

Merrick and Mike looked at each other for a moment or two and then started to laugh. But if Merrick had responded affirmatively to Kippy's offer, I have absolutely no doubt about the fate that would have befallen Jerry Robbins. That's the kind of staunch friend Kippy was. Or, come to think of it, maybe he just wanted to get a laugh out of Merrick.

Bob Fosse was one of the theater's most talented choreographer-directors. His will included a clause that provided funds for a dinner for his friends upon his demise. When his lawyer told him that a Hollywood producer's will had a similar clause, Fosse said, "However much he's provided, make mine $10,000 more."

On the eve of his emergency quadruple bypass heart surgery, which Fosse immortalized in his motion picture *All That Jazz*, playwrights Paddy Chayefsky and Herb Gardner, his two best friends, were summoned to the hospital to witness his will. Gardner signed the will without looking at any but the last of its thirty or more pages. But Chayefsky insisted on reading through all of it.

"But I'm not even mentioned in the

will," Chayefsky said to Fosse, who was in bed, heavily sedated. Fosse smiled weakly and shook his head.

"Fuck you!" said Chayefsky. "Live!"

○●○●○

On the road and out of town

○●○●○

---○---

Bill Doll, one of the theater's legendary press agents, was with a show trying out in Philadelphia. When the first-time producer complained that the play's title was misspelled on the theater's marquee, Doll, the veteran, looked disdainfully at the parvenu and said, spacing his words out very slowly and deliberately, "That's why shows go out of town."

---○---

*P*EOPLE OF THE Broadway theater have always tended to view the rest of this country with a measure of geocentric disdain: anything beyond the Hudson River is either "out of town" or "the road." To theater folk such cities as Boston, Philadelphia, Baltimore, and Washington, D.C., are "out of town," there for no other purpose than to provide the theaters and audiences so that plays and musicals can be tried out before they reach Broadway.

"The road" is something quite different. Many of us have spent a lot of time through the years on "the road"—touring the length and breadth of this land, as I have, in plays and musicals. I have found that the road can be dangerous. A few of my friends—Bob Crane of *Hogan's Heroes* was one—have been murdered on the road. This is not just an expression. I am not talking about what the critics did to them. I mean murdered. And in no case was the murderer found.

When I first went into the theater, the road was still very much alive. In Tulsa it was what I grew up on. We saw the road companies of all the hits, often pale copies of the originals. But, for example, when Katharine Cornell came through in *Romeo and Juliet* it was with a better company than she had had on Broadway. Maurice Evans was Romeo and Ralph Richardson was Mercutio, both making their American debuts—not in New York, but on the road. Tyrone Power was

Benvolio and the dances were staged by Martha Graham. I remember Walter Huston came through Tulsa in *Dodsworth* and Walter Hampden showed up in repertory —*Cyrano, Hamlet*—almost every year.

When I was going to Northwestern, the Chicago theater was flourishing. The Loop had seventeen legitimate theaters and the Chicago company of a Broadway hit was in every one of them. Louis Calhern and Lillian Gish, for example, were in *Life with Father.* Some people thought they were better than the Broadway originals.

And yet the road has always had this connotation of second-rate. Some of the old timers like George Cukor used the word *road* as a pejorative. "Oh, don't do that," he'd sometimes say when he directed me in *Let's Make Love,* a picture I did with Marilyn Monroe, "it's terribly road."

The playwright and actor Howard Lindsay *("Life with Father,"* etc.) told me that in his young days when he was the manager of a stock company, a famous actress who had a serious drinking problem was playing there. Her daughter was her dresser, and in charge of portioning out just enough liquor to get her through every performance. You can almost always tell when an actor's drunk. He speaks very slowly, trying very hard to appear sober, and becomes terribly serious. On this particular night she was slower than ever and Lindsay went backstage to talk to her.

"I must speak to you about this. Your speech was very slow tonight."

"Well, you see, Mr. Lindsay," she said, pointing to her mouth, "these are my road teeth."

I was with Katharine Cornell on her last tour in *The Barretts of Wimpole Street.* Maureen Stapleton was Wilson, the maid, Anne Jackson was in it, and I played Elizabeth's stuttering brother. And the great English actor Wilfrid Lawson played Elizabeth's father, Mr. Barrett. Cornell always said it was the best company she'd ever had in the play. No one could ever equal—come close, in fact—to Wilfrid Lawson. He was the best actor I've ever been onstage with. In fact Peter Smith is writing a biography of him now called *The Best of Us All.* Peter O'Toole, Richard Burton, Albert Finney, and their generation of British actors worshiped him, not only for his extraordinary acting but for his prodigious drinking powers. His role in the movie of *Pygmalion* as Liza's besotted father was typecasting. Even though Lawson was sometimes drunk onstage on the *Barretts* tour, he was always astonishing in the part. J. B. Priestley said to me one night in New York, "I've had them all in my plays—Olivier, Gielgud, Richardson —but the best of them all was Lawson." He was a character actor, of course, whose gnarled little physique kept him from playing the great roles.

Out of town is quite another matter. Until recently, shows never opened "cold" on Broadway. You always went out of town with a play or a musical until the producer thought it was ready to "bring in." Sometimes they decide not to and close

○ 81 ○

the show out of town. Sometimes you wish the producer had.

I was sent *UTBU,* a new play by Jimmy Kirkwood. I read it and thought it was one of the funniest plays I'd ever read. I had to do it! Thelma Ritter and Alan Webb were in it and Nancy Walker was set to direct. The play got less and less funny as we rehearsed it, which sometimes happens. It just wouldn't play. We begged the producer not to open it, but open we did, in Boston, and it was hopeless. When we got to Philadelphia in late December there was, to our astonishment, a line around the theater. "How," I asked myself, "could I have been so wrong?" What I soon discovered is that the people were on line to get their money back. They had all read the Boston reviews! We played a matinee on Christmas Day and there were about twelve people in the audience. At the curtain call I shouted, "Merry Christmas!" to the audience and someone shouted back, "Go to hell!" The foolhardy producer opened the show in New York at the Helen Hayes Theatre and we closed three days later. Some years later I became active in the struggle to save the Helen Hayes and other theaters from the developers' wrecking balls. "This theater," I said in an impassioned speech I made at a rally in front of the Helen Hayes, "housed the biggest flop I was ever in!"

Moss Hart, the playwright and director, was out of town in Washington, D.C., with a play that was in a lot of trouble. The next stop, if there was to be one, was Broadway.

Hart, his younger brother, Bernie, who was functioning as the stage manager, the playwright, and several others on the creative staff were in one of those desperate all-night sessions in Hart's hotel suite. Bernie was contributing nothing whatsoever to the meeting.

"Bernie," Hart said, "we're in a lot of trouble and you haven't said a word. Somehow we've got to get it all together and get out of here in two weeks."

"Don't worry, Moss," Bernie said in a

very calm and reassuring tone, "we got out of Egypt, we'll get out of Washington."

Moss Hart, it seemed to me, was one of the most glamorous men in the theater. Max Gordon was producing a new Hart play and sent me to meet him. I went to his beautiful town house and Hart, a very handsome, elegant man, welcomed me warmly as he descended a magnificent staircase. Some years later I told his widow, Kitty Carlisle Hart, how I always remembered meeting Moss in their beautiful town house. "But," she said, "we never had a town house. We never had a staircase." I guess I put him in one because he seemed so glamorous to me. That, I suppose, is how stories become apocryphal.

When a musical is out of town and in trouble, the rewriting and restaging are done under enormous pressure. Fixing a musical and getting it ready for Broadway can be the most complicated, difficult, exasperating, and maddening of all theatrical endeavors. Tempers, as a consequence, are at their shortest, nerves their most frayed, and temperamental personalities are at their most conflicting.

An especially harrowing pre-Broadway experience with *The Conquering Hero* moved the show's librettist, Larry Gelbart, to say, "If Hitler's alive I hope he's out of town with a musical."

When a musical comedy is being revised out of town, it is often decided that what's needed is a brand-new, show-stopping number. The composer thereupon leaves wherever it is that the producer, director, choreographer, *et al.,* have forgathered and a half hour later, much to everyone's amazement, he returns, sits down at the piano, and plays a song that dazzles everyone. How does he do it?

According to Cy Feuer, the veteran producer of many Broadway musical hits including *Guys and Dolls,* the explanation is really quite simple. It's what he calls *"Eine Kleine Trunk Musik."*

Sometimes the opposite is decided— that is, cut a musical number that isn't working. That was the case on *Oh Captain.* When we were in Philadelphia we were thirty minutes too long and we had to cut songs and dances and parts of the book. A fellow actor and I were backstage reading through the cuts when I heard him say very quietly, "I'm out of the show." Unfortunately, that's the cruel way in which things sometimes happen in the theater.

Cy Feuer and Ernie Martin, the producers, Bob Fosse, the director, Cy Coleman, the composer, and Neil Simon, the book writer, were all in agreement that a musical number in *Little Me* had to be cut. Carolyn Leigh, the lyricist, was the lone dissenter. The song was cut despite her vehement protestations. That night, after the show, Leigh went out on the streets of Philadelphia and found a policeman standing in front of the theater.

"Come with me," she said.

Leigh, accompanied by the cop, pointed at her collaborators, who were having a meeting backstage, and said in deadly earnest, "I want you to arrest these men!"

"What did you do to this lady?" the cop asked.

"We cut her song," Feuer replied.

Starting with *On the Town,* Adolph Green, my neighbor, and Betty Comden have written the book and/or lyrics of a long string of successful Broadway musicals. One recent evening at a theater in New York a man greeted Betty, who couldn't quite place him.

"But don't you remember? I was in the chorus of *Bonanza Bound.*"

That was the one Comden and Green musical that never made it to New York. It had opened and closed in Philadelphia some twenty-five years before.

"Oh, of course," Betty said. "How are you?"

"I'm fine," he replied. "Do you remember that night in Philly after the final performance? We were all feeling so down and you and Adolph got us all together onstage and told us how you were going to rewrite the show, bring us all back into rehearsal, go out of town again, and then bring it to Broadway."

"Yes," she replied, "of course I do."

"Well, I was wondering if it would be all right if I went out now and got another job!"

Sydney Chaplin, son of Charlie, was in Philadelphia for the pre-Broadway try-out of still another Comden and Green musical, *Subways Are for Sleeping.* It was blasted by the critics. While Betty and Adolph were at their hotel working feverishly on rewrites with the director, Michael Kidd, the company was being rehearsed at the theater by the show's composer, Jule Styne. He stopped the rehearsal in the middle of a scene and asked Chaplin to repeat a line that the actor had mumbled. Chaplin repeated the line and Styne, a very excitable little man, stopped the rehearsal again.

"Sydney, I still can't understand what you're saying. Please say it again."

"I'm not saying that line," Sydney responded.

"What do you mean you're not saying that line?"

"It's a terrible line and I'm not saying it."

"I've never heard an actor say anything so unprofessional," Styne sputtered.

"Listen, Jule," Chaplin said to his longtime friend, "I have $750,000 in the bank that my father gave me and there's nothing in the world that's going to make me say that line."

Styne was flabbergasted. "Do you mean to tell me that if you were poor you'd say the line?"

"If I were poor, Julie, I'd suck your cock!"

Jule Styne and Sammy Cahn were out of town with their new musical *Glad to See Ya,* and, of course, it was in a lot of trouble. To make matters even worse, its leading man, who didn't as yet have an understudy, got sick and Cahn had to go on for him.

One night when things were at their worst, Styne told Cahn that George Abbott, the director, playwright, and most skillful of all play doctors, was out front. "I'll ask him what he thinks we should do."

Styne went into Cahn's dressing room after the performance.

"So what did Mr. Abbott say?"

"He said take the end and put it at the beginning."

" 'Take the end and put it at the beginning'? What the hell does that mean?"

"I don't know, but that's what he said and that's what I think we should do."

The show closed out of town.

Several years later Styne and Cahn wrote the score of *High Button Shoes,* which Mr. Abbott directed. During a rehearsal Cahn had a minor dispute with Mr. Abbott, as he is known to all of us in the theater. Cahn said, "I know, I know— 'take the end and put it at the beginning.' "

Mr. Abbott looked at Cahn blankly. "What are you talking about, Sammy?"

"That's what you told Jule we should do when you came to see *Glad to See Ya.*"

"I never saw that show."

"You didn't?"

"Absolutely not."

Cahn caught up with Styne later.

"Mr. Abbott tells me he never saw *Glad to See Ya.* How come you told me he was there and said, 'Take the end and put it at the beginning'?"

"Because if *I* had told you that's what we should do, would you have listened to me?"

Busby Berkeley, the choreographer of *42nd Street* and many other spectacular Hollywood movie musicals, was brought in to try to save *Glad to See Ya.* During rehearsals he kept telling one of the actors to move farther and farther upstage.

"If he moves any farther back," one of his assistants commented, "no one will be able to see him."

"Oh, don't worry," said Berkeley, who had a movie director's viewfinder up to his eye, "I'll move in on him."

Mike Nichols was having problems out of town with Walter Matthau during a rehearsal of *The Odd Couple.* The actor was not giving the director the interpretation he wanted and Nichols wasn't at all happy about it. He was finally forced to chew out the actor in front of the cast and crew.

"And if you don't like it," Nichols said in conclusion, "then you can leave."

"All right," the humiliated Matthau said, "but before I go, give me my balls back."

Without hesitating Nichols turned and shouted offstage, "Props!"

I think the most famous of all out-of-town stories must be the one about Cy Howard, the comedy writer *(My Friend Irma, Life with Luigi),* who was asked by his friend Al Bloomingdale, of the department-store family, to take a look at a show he was backing that was in trouble in Philadelphia. Howard offered Bloomingdale the following advice:

"Close the show and keep the store open nights."

Philadelphia, I know, is beginning to sound like the Cape Hatteras of the theater. David Merrick has had more than one show in Philly that's been in trouble. Tom Snyder, then working for a local TV station, was assigned to interview members of the audience as they left the theater on the opening night of this particular Merrick production. Merrick, very concerned about the show's future, didn't want him to. (Perhaps Merrick was inspired by Sam Goldwyn, who said after a disastrous sneak preview of one of his films, "There's got to be some way of stopping the word of mouth on this picture!") Merrick, as he usually does, prevailed. He arranged to have the cable of the remote camera severed. When the TV station threatened to sue for damages, he sent them a roll of electrician's tape.

Just one more story about a show trying out in Philadelphia and then I'll be done with it. Otto Preminger, the ofttimes despotic Teutonic director, was making everyone's life so miserable that the cast and crew decided to send him a letter of protest. If everyone in the company signed it, they reasoned, he couldn't retaliate.

Everyone signed it except for one actor. "I still have relatives living in Germany!"

○ 93 ○

Groucho Marx summed up the infinite delights of the theater best when he and I were sitting together in a dressing room at the Booth Theatre for a Tony Awards broadcast. All the men from all the Broadway shows were in this one dressing room, and in another room across the way were the chorus girls from all the Broadway musicals. They left the door open and you could see some of them running around stark naked.

Groucho leaned over to me and said, "You don't get this in the pants business."

4

○●○○●○

Hollywood

at

home

○●○○●○

---○---

Hollywood was once an El Dorado where almost everyone was making enormous sums of money. Staying in touch with reality often wasn't easy in tinsel town. Joseph Pasternak, a producer, was looking at costume sketches for the female star of his latest production.

"No, no," said Pasternak to the designer, "these are all much too fancy. She plays a schoolteacher, for Christ's sake—someone who's never earned more than $1000 a week in her life."

---○---

O NE OF THE real regrets of my life is that by the time I arrived in Hollywood the golden days were pretty much a thing of the past. Or perhaps it just seemed that way to someone who wasn't around during those glamorous, "more - stars - than - there - are - in - heaven" years when the town was ruled as the personal fiefdoms of a handful of despots.

I got to Hollywood in 1957 when I made *Oh Men! Oh Women!* for Twentieth Century-Fox. It was thanks to Nunnally Johnson, a jewel among men, that I got the part.

There have been maybe a half-dozen men who've really made a difference in my career, who came along and gave me that big push at a time when I needed it. Nunnally was one of them. He'd seen me on Broadway in *Inherit the Wind.* He'd also seen me in the Broadway production of *Oh, Men! Oh, Women!* but fortunately, he didn't remember. He'd seen it with the original cast when it first opened, fallen in love with it, and wanted to do it as a movie. He came back to see it again but, he told me, the cast wasn't nearly as good. I kept my mouth shut because I had re-placed Gig Young!

My first day ever in front of a movie camera was in New York. We were filming the exteriors of *Oh Men! Oh Women!* on a luxury liner, the *Île de France,* which was docked in the Hudson. I sat down in a deck chair and waited for Nunnally, the director, to call me. The ship's steward brought me a martini and I sat back and enjoyed the sun. At lunch the ship's superb French chef prepared one of the greatest meals I can ever remember eating. It included champagne and a baked Alaska for dessert. After lunch I went back to my deck chair, had a brandy, and fell asleep. At almost the end of the day I was summoned by Nunnally, who, in that courteous southern way of his, asked me to run down the gangplank, which I did. And that was it. They sent me home. This is movies? I thought. But this is wonderful! I was nearly forty years old, I had never made a movie, and I had one of the most pleasant days of my life. This is for me!

Say what you will about those true, first-generation pioneers—most notably Louis B. Mayer of MGM, Columbia's Harry Cohn, Sam Goldwyn, and Jack L. Warner, whose studio introduced "talkies"—they were completely dedicated to motion pictures, unlike the people who are running things now—agents, lawyers, deal makers. The entrenched establishment of today got rid of David Puttnam, the last picture maker to run a studio—Columbia—in a hurry. Jokes were made about Goldwyn and the things he allegedly said—"An oral contract isn't worth the paper it's written on"—but just think of the great pictures he made. And the talents he had working on them! The absolute best, like George Balanchine, whom he hired to choreograph *The Goldwyn Follies.* Balanchine imposed one condition: He was to be given three weeks of rehearsals with the dancers, including his wife, ballerina Vera Zorina, who was starring in the film. No one, Goldwyn included, was to be allowed on the rehearsal stage. After two weeks of noninterference Goldwyn could not stand it any longer. He summoned Balanchine to his office.

"I've given you everything you asked for, Mr. Balanchine. I wouldn't dream of violating the terms of our agreement, but I would at least like to have some idea of what I will be getting for my money."

With the graceful flourish of the dancer he always was, Balanchine picked up a pencil from Goldwyn's desk and put it down. He then said, in an accent that was even thicker than Goldwyn's, "Major." Balanchine then picked up a letter opener, which he placed beside the pencil.

"Minor," he said. "First movement."

After a pregnant pause Balanchine continued. "Second movement," he said.

He turned the pencil around and placed the letter opener across it.

"Minor."

He paused pregnantly once again and resumed.

"Third movement—major."

He moved the pencil an inch and removed the letter opener.

"Minor."

Balanchine looked up at Goldwyn, who was beaming.

"I like it!"

That's not what Goldwyn said when

Billy Wilder, the writer-director, was pitching him a Nijinsky project. Wilder told him all about the legendary Russian ballet dancer who left his lover, Diaghilev, the impresario, for a woman, whom he married, and how he eventually became hopelessly insane and lived out his life in a Swiss asylum, where he completely lost touch with reality and thought he was a horse.

"How dare you even suggest that I make a picture like that?"

"Look," said Wilder as he was being ejected from Goldwyn's office, "if you want a happy ending, we could have him win the Kentucky Derby."

From all I've ever heard, Harry Cohn must've been the most despised studio head in the history of Hollywood.

When Cohn died, a producer who had worked for him at Columbia was asked if he intended to go to the funeral.

"Not unless they're burying him alive."

I am not going to repeat the oft-told story about the remark made at the funeral and most often attributed to Red Skelton. "You see," Red said when he saw how crowded it was, "give the public what it wants . . ."

MEMO

From: Jack L. Warner
To: Executive Staff

It's time I started thinking about the possibility of someone replacing me as the studio's head of production. I need your help. If there is any such qualified person presently working at the studio, I want him fired.

Warner was only slightly less despotic than Cohn. When he was asked why he had fired an executive who had been with the studio for more than thirty years, he replied, "Things just weren't working out."

As for working conditions in general at Warner Bros., Wilson Mizner described them best:

"It's like two porcupines mating: one prick against a thousand others."

Mizner said of Harry Warner that he had his suits made with oilcloth pockets for stealing soup.

Adolph Zukor, the founder of Paramount Pictures, outlived all of the other industry pioneers, whose average life span, for reasons unknown, rivaled that of symphony conductors. At his hundredth birthday celebration Zukor said, "If I had known I was going to live this long, I would've taken better care of myself."

Irving Thalberg, the head of production at MGM, died young. Harry Carey, who had an up-and-down career as an actor in Hollywood, was amazed when he received an invitation to be a pallbearer at Thalberg's funeral. He had never met Thalberg. From then on his career went straight back to the top. He never stopped working for the rest of his life. What had happened is that Thalberg's secretary meant to send the invitation to Thalberg's closest friend, the screenwriter Carey Wilson.

Thalberg, who was the head of a studio when he was nineteen, was a great producer, possibly the best that Hollywood has ever had, a man of genius. Such disparate people as Groucho Marx and John Barrymore always spoke of him in the highest terms. However, he had one failing as an executive—he didn't like to fire people. One day he nevertheless did actually fire one writer. That same night Thalberg went to visit what my mother used to call a "friend" who lived in one of those Hollywood patio apartment houses where you climbed stairs and walked around a balcony to the door. Thalberg went to the wrong door and this writer whom he had fired that day opened it. "I felt so bad about firing you," Thalberg said, "that I came to tell you that you've got your job back."

Darryl Zanuck, although not a pioneer, ranked in power with all the other industry moguls and he was the last of them. From all I've ever heard, he was a sexual athlete. He was chasing Judy Holliday around his office at Twentieth Century-Fox and when he caught up with her, he pushed her down onto a couch. Defending herself as best she could, Judy pointed to a framed photograph of Zanuck's wife and three children.

"How could you?" Holliday said. "There's your family."

Deeply offended, Zanuck stood up, walked away, and said, "Keep my family out of this."

Bella Darvi, a European actress, had a modest career on the silver screen thanks entirely to Zanuck's infatuation with her. Darvi was a name bestowed on her by the studio, a combination of the first three letters of *Darryl* and the first two letters of his wife *Virginia*'s name. Creating new names for actors and actresses was a common practice in those days. Tony Curtis, for example, was Bernie Schwartz when he was signed to a long-term contract by Universal. The studio had a contest to find him a new name. Shelley Winters suggested they change it to Al Schwartz.

John Garfield was in a New York restaurant and a waitress came over to him and said, "Don't I know you?" to which he replied, "Could be." She shook her head, walked away, and leaned against a wall and stared at him. And then she came back and said, "But I know you from someplace." "Could be." "I've got it! Julie Garfinkle, P.S. 23."

By the time George Segal got to Hollywood the name-changing practice had stopped.

I gather no one in the Hollywood community could understand the enormous hold that Darvi had over Zanuck.

"It's really quite simple," Nunnally Johnson explained. "Bella took him to bed and until then he thought it was something you did on top of a desk."

Nunnally, a superb screenwriter, never became a top-flight director. I would say that all of the really good motion-picture directors are extremely controlling men—they really have to be. But Nunnally was much too easygoing. He was also the producer of *Oh Men! Oh Women!* and occasionally he had to do whatever the hell it is that producers do. One day he said to all of us in that charming southern drawl of his, "Ah've got to go to mah office. I hate to do it but it's im-pawhtant. So y'all rehearse the scene while ahm gone and if it's any good, why, go right ahead and shoot it."

John Ford, it seems, was the most controlling of all directors. Directors al-ways get as much coverage—the master shot, the two-shots, over the shoulders, and close-ups—as many angles as they possibly can, so that when they finish shooting and go into the cutting room they have the luxury of composing every scene in as many ways as possible until it's the way they want it. Not John Ford. In the days when directors did not have the right of final cut, Ford shot his pictures with no protection at all, so that when he was finished there was only one way it could be put together. No meddlesome studio head was going to recut Ford's pic-tures.

When Ford began shooting *The In-former,* he introduced the producer, Cliff Reid, to the assembled cast and crew.

"Take a good look at him," Ford said,

"because you won't be seeing him again for fourteen days."

Just imagine—*The Informer,* a screen masterpiece—shot in fourteen days!

On the fourteenth day Reid walked onto the set. Ford stopped everything.

"What are you doing here?"

"Well," the producer began, "inasmuch as it's the last day, I thought—"

"It's now no longer the last day," Ford said.

And just for spite Ford added an extra day to the schedule.

George Stevens was Ford's opposite. At the first sneak of one of his masterpieces, *Shane,* the audience's reaction was very poor.

"I know what's wrong with it," Stevens told the studio executives who had assembled under the theater's marquee for the postmortem. "The story should be told from the little boy's point of view."

"I'm not going to pay to have you go back and shoot all that footage" said Y. Frank Freeman, the head of Paramount Pictures.

"No, no," Stevens said, "I have all that footage. I just have to reedit."

I'm quite sure that if Stevens had decided after the sneak that the story should've been told from the horse's point of view, he would've had that footage too.

All of the good directors I have worked with and know about are resolute and are going to get what they want one way or another.

When Vincente Minnelli, who was, I understand, the mildest and gentlest of men, was directing *The Sandpiper,* Richard Burton and Elizabeth Taylor, for complicated tax reasons, could not spend a day more than three weeks in the States to shoot the exteriors. The very last scene scheduled was at a school outside Los Angeles. Burton, as the headmaster, was to be in the foreground of the shot going over remodeling plans with an architect. In the very distant background Elizabeth Taylor was to come into the shot as a passenger in a small pickup truck loaded with farm produce and a crate of chickens. Minnelli arrived at the location and saw that the chickens in the crate were Rhode Island reds. "But," he said to the head of the prop department, "I want white leghorns."

"Vincente," the production manager said, "no one's going to see them. What difference does it make?"

But it made a big difference to Minnelli, a former scenic designer, who always placed great emphasis on the visual. And so the prop department spent several hours combing the environs for white leghorns while Burton and Taylor, bemused and incredulous, waited. No matter what, scene or no scene, they were leaving the country the next day. Minnelli showed not the slightest sign of concern or pressure, as he calmly sat in his canvas-backed director's chair humming to himself as he so often did.

The propmen came back without the white leghorns. At that point another director, less strong willed, might've made the Rhode Island reds do. But not Minnelli. He was determined to have white chickens in the crate, and white chickens he got. The chickens were held upside down by their legs and as they cackled crazily and flapped their wings frantically, the propmen sprayed them with white paint.

I worked with an old-time director, George Marshall, on *The Mating Game,* a film I did at MGM with Debbie Reynolds. He was about 70 and it was his 404th film! His career spanned almost the entire history of movies. He made his first movie in 1916 and directed over two hundred Laurel and Hardy shorts! He didn't want any suggestions from anyone on the set. Whenever Phil Barry, Jr., the producer, came down to the set and said anything, Marshall would sort of laugh and say, "You're thinking again." He was a mean old goat but he was one of the great masters of screen comedy *(Destry Rides Again, The Sheepman,* etc.), with a remarkably fertile comedic mind. He'd make up gags every day while we were on the set. He wouldn't even let you rehearse. He'd think of a physical gag and work it out on his feet. He'd say something like "You walk in the door, you let the door hit you in the face, you fall down and roll over." And he'd do it. You'd watch this old man who had trouble walking do it a few times until he got it right and then he'd say, "Okay, let's shoot it!"

We had a very funny scene where I'm on the phone—drunk—talking to my boss. I remember the scene ended with my saying, "Roger, Dodger, old codger." We shot the scene. It was in the can. Two weeks later, shooting schedules being what they are, we were shooting the scene that leads up to the phone scene. We were about halfway through it when suddenly the script girl—I remember her name was Rose Steinberg—let out an "Oh, my God!" as if someone had dropped a snake in her lap. "What's the matter?" Marshall asked her. "In the scene when Tony's on the phone, he doesn't have a tie on. And in this scene, which we've half shot, he has a tie on. They don't match. We'll have to reshoot this scene." But nothing threw old George. We still hadn't shot the little bit where the phone rings and I make a cross to pick it up. So Marshall says to me, "Tony, as the phone rings and you run across the room to pick it up, take off your tie." I said, "What in the world are you talking about, George? What's my reason for taking off my tie?" And he said, "Don't ask stupid questions. Just take it off as you're running and throw it in the air." There was no time to argue. The tie had to come off. I did exactly what he told me to do. I took the tie off and threw it in the air with mad abandon. And it's one of the big laughs in the film.

I had a scene in *Let's Make Love,* which another true Hollywood master, George Cukor, was directing. It consisted of me coming in, sitting down in a chair, and waiting. So I ambled in—I had a raincoat on—started to sit down—decided to take my raincoat off—then I decided to leave it on—then I didn't like where the chair was and decided to move it a few inches with my foot—then I looked in my pocket for my newspaper to read and realized it was in my inside pocket—then I decided the light wasn't so good so I looked around for a better light to read by —and then I started to look for my glasses —and then Cukor screamed at me, "Why don't you have a heart attack?" I had stretched what should've been one foot of film into an entire scene! I just kept finding things to do. And that's what acting is. If you have a guy who'll just walk in and sit down, you know he ain't no actor. An actor wants to find everything there is in each moment—that's an actor's instinct. To try to be real. To try to find the physical reality. A director's job is to select from what the actor offers him—the million things that an inventive actor has given him to choose from.

David Lean, surely one of the world's finest directors, is a meticulous and fastidious craftsman, compulsive and uncompromising about getting things exactly the way he wants them. There is a scene in *Summertime* in which Isa Miranda, who plays the owner of the Venetian pensione in which Katharine Hepburn is staying, arranges a tryst with Darren McGavin, a young American guest. The entire scene takes place at night on the terrace of the pensione overlooking the Grand Canal.

Lean put Miranda and McGavin in two high-backed wicker chairs that completely enveloped them. What's more, the chairs were placed with their backs to the camera so that all the lens could see were her left hand holding his right hand and puffs of white smoke from the cigarettes curling above the backs of the chairs. The brief scene, which could have been shot with any two people sitting in the chairs and the voices of Miranda and McGavin dubbed in later, took an entire night and a carton of cigarettes to film. Lean made the two actors do it over and over. Just as dawn was about to break, Lean finally got a take that satisfied him.

"Perfect! Perfect!" Lean exclaimed enthusiastically. "The puffs were perfect!"

If he had done that to me I think I might've punched him. As for the smoking, I'll do it if the scene calls for it but it makes me sick.

After completing the principal photography Lean remained in Venice with a camera crew shooting what's known as pickup shots. In his never-ending quest for perfection and a general reluctance he shares with most other directors ever to finish filming, Lean would probably still be in Venice if the producer, Ilya Lopert, hadn't closed the production's bank account.

Robert Rossen, the very gifted director and writer of such films as *All the King's Men, Body and Soul,* and *The Hustler,* was as tough as any director I've ever heard about. The very last words Mike heard him utter were at a New Year's Day party he and his wife, Sue, gave. Rossen had just finished what turned out to be his last picture, *Lilith,* on which, it seems, the film's costar, Warren Beatty, had created all kinds of difficulties for Rossen. Just as Mike was leaving the party, Rossen, seated in an armchair and looking very frail and feeble, motioned for him to come to his side. He was quite obviously a dying man. Mike bent down and heard Rossen, feisty to the end, say in the faintest of voices, "If I ever get better, I'm going to kill Warren Beatty!"

Mike, and Alfred Katz, a publicist, befriended Rossen when he was blacklisted by the industry and unable to work. There were times during this agonizing period when Rossen, frustrated and demoralized, could be very difficult.

"Gee, Bob," Katz said to Rossen during one of his more unpleasant moods, "I wish you'd get back on your feet so we could drop you."

I had a rather sad experience with Mike Gordon, the director, the day we began *Pillow Talk*. The first scene scheduled to be shot was one I had objected to. There were certain jokes in it that I found most objectionable because they made psychiatry and psychiatrists look ridiculous. I had been promised that it would be rewritten. When I asked Mike for the new pages he said, "I don't know anything about it. I've got to shoot this scene." I said I wouldn't do it and so at eleven o'clock in the morning he broke us for lunch.

○ 118 ○

I went into the commissary and sat there picking at something and presently the picture's producer, Ross Hunter, came up to me and said, "What are you trying to do?"

"What do you mean?"

"Are you trying to destroy that man?"

"I was promised rewrites of those pages."

"That has nothing to do with it," Ross said. "This is the first day Mike has worked in five years. He's been blacklisted. And you practically destroyed him in front of the entire crew. If you destroy him now he'll probably never work again for the rest of his life."

You can imagine how I felt. I'd been looking at it only from my point of view. I don't much believe in a private apology for a public insult, and so after lunch I went back onto the set and in front of the same people I apologized. Mike threw his arms around me and I've never been able to get them off. He's been one of my best friends ever since.

They always put up a little office on

the set for the director—four flats with a desk, a chair, and a cot. Mike Curtiz, the director of *Casablanca* and *The Charge of the Light Brigade,* had an extra in there one day doing what used to be known as a "very special favor" for him. As Curtiz luxuriated in his pleasure, he leaned back, looked up, and saw four or five stagehands looking down at him from a catwalk above the soundstage. "Crazy girl!" Curtiz said with his Hungarian quickness. "Vot are you doing?"

I knew it was a true story because when I worked for Mike I asked him if it was and he replied, "Oh, Hal Wallis made it up to embarrass me."

William Wyler, a director I have always admired enormously, is often confused by the public with Billy Wilder. One of Hollywood's most honored directors, Wyler made such outstanding pictures as *Wuthering Heights, Ben-Hur, The Best Years of Our Lives, The Little Foxes,* and *Roman Holiday,* for which he won a total of four Academy Awards. Of all the questions asked of him by neophyte directors,

Wyler said the most intelligent by far was put to him by Mike Nichols on the eve of starting his first picture, *Who's Afraid of Virginia Woolf?* Nichols introduced himself to the master at a Hollywood cocktail party and said, "There's a question I must ask you." Wyler braced himself as Nichols continued. "What do you wear when you're directing?"

Wyler is a rare example of someone in show business who actually chose to retire voluntarily, something, I might add, I never intend to do. He spent the rest of his life traveling with his lovely wife, Talli, to various parts of the world, often to film festivals at which he was honored with retrospectives of his distinguished work. At dinner in their Beverly Hills home a guest said, "Willie, you've been everywhere. Is there someplace you haven't been that you'd like to see?"

Wyler considered the question for a few moments, and replied, "Yes, downtown Los Angeles."

David Niven, with whom I worked on *Oh Men! Oh Women!* told me a lot of William *Wyler* stories. Niven—who told almost all of his great stories in those wonderful books of his—and Keenan Wynn, and José Ferrer, and Guthrie McClintic were the best storytellers there ever were. Ferrer, of course, is still very much alive, but Niven, Wynn, and McClintic should have been preserved forever so no one else could tell the world's great stories.

Known as "Wild Willie" before he settled down and got married, Wyler wasn't terribly articulate around actors. Rather than explain his intentions he simply had them do a scene over and over again until he got what he wanted. He supposedly had Laurence Olivier walk down some stairs in *Wuthering Heights* more than forty times. Olivier quite understandably became a little impatient, as I certainly would have, and asked Wyler to please tell him exactly what he wanted.

"When you do it right, I'll tell you."

But actors, especially Bette Davis, loved to work with Willie because somehow they always gave their best performances in Wyler pictures. Niven, who always spoke to me about Wyler with enormous affection and admiration, said that Wyler once humiliated him in front of the entire *Wuthering Heights* company. It was in the scene in which Merle Oberon as Cathy is on her deathbed and Niven, her heartbroken husband, is kneeling at her side. They rehearsed the scene and then as they were about to shoot it, Wyler told Niven that he wanted him to cry. Niven took Wyler aside and confided to him, very quietly, that he couldn't cry. Wyler didn't believe him at first, but Niven assured him that he wasn't kidding.

"Do you mean to tell me that you, a professional actor, can't cry?" Wyler, normally a quiet man, roared. Niven tried to quiet him down but Wyler persisted.

"I don't believe it," Wyler said for all the cast and crew to hear. "Here's an actor who can't cry!"

As David told me, he asked all the other actors how they cry and they all told him: Think of the saddest thing you know and then start to cry. So Niven did. He thought of the death of his dog when he was a boy and very soon great heaving sobs started but no tears came; only, as he so delicately described it, "great gobs of green slime" ran out of his nose and hung there. Wyler decided to shoot Niven in this scene from the back.

David told me there was a relatively minor, insignificant cut in *Wuthering Heights* that Sam Goldwyn would never let Wyler make. It always bothered him. Years and many pictures later Wyler was running the movie and when he got to that scene, he ordered the projectionist to stop. Willie went into the booth and had the projectionist make the cut in the print. However many years later that was, the director had his way.

And then there were the journeymen directors like Lloyd Bacon. Oscar Levant was acting in one of his pictures and asked him what kind of a reading he wanted on a certain line.

"Oscar, I wish you wouldn't ask me questions like that."

*　*　*

Except for the director and cameraman, picture making can be the most excruciatingly boring experience known to man, especially for the actors who just sit around forever with nothing to do while they light the next setup. But when Niven was around, it was something else. He kept everyone laughing, alert, and alive. One day he had Dan Dailey, who was also in *Oh Men! Oh Women!* with us, laughing so hard his face became the color of an eggplant and he had to be re–made up.

David once said to me—and I'm going to change the star's name—"Now, promise me you won't repeat this, old boy —not to anyone—but Mona was the best there ever was. The best! You could be in bed with Mona—now, Tony, I do have your promise that you won't breathe a word of this to anyone—but you could be in bed with Mona and at a particular moment you might have a fleeting, unexpressed notion that you'd like to take a mackerel, wrap it in newspaper, and shove it up her ass. And, dear boy, without your saying a word to her, she'd get up out of bed, go downstairs to the kitchen, and come back with a fish!"

Oh, what a delight David was.

In the days of the all-powerful studio heads, many producers were little more than figureheads.

George Jessel, a Zanuck crony and court jester in residence at the studio, was on the payroll at Fox as a producer. He had no illusions about his responsibilities and authority. On the first day of production on a picture to which he had been assigned, Jessel assembled the director, cast, and crew and said, "Okay, I'll see you all again at the first sneak preview."

There were exceptions, of course. Hal Wallis for one. He was the head of production at Warner Bros. in its heyday, second in command to Jack. He then became an enormously successful independent producer. When he was starting out in the business, he married Louise Fazenda, one of the silent screen's reigning queens. Wallis was known around town as the Prisoner of Fazenda.

Wallis's sister Minna, an agent, was never known for her beauty. Her looks, in fact, were the butt of many unkind jokes, the cruelest but without doubt the funniest of which was, of course, Billy Wilder's. Wilder concocted a scenario for a science-fiction movie about an enormous erection that was invading the United States. As it approached our shores, it grew bigger and bigger, harder and harder. Machine-gun and artillery fire, bombs, flame throwers —nothing could stop it. In desperation the Joint Chiefs convened. The very future of the nation was at stake. Their decision?

"Send for Minna Wallis."

Arthur Freed had his own unit at MGM and produced some of the best musicals ever made in Hollywood: *An American in Paris, Gigi,* and *Singin' in the Rain* among them. Freed, who was also a very gifted songwriter, had an overwhelming need to impress.

Saul Chaplin, who left Columbia to join the Freed unit as an arranger and associate producer, and Oscar Levant were watching a live Dodger game on television when Freed dropped in on them.

"Do you want to watch the game with us, Arthur?" Chaplin asked his boss.

"Oh, no, thanks," Freed replied. "I've seen it. Louis B. Mayer ran it last night at his house."

Eddie Feldman, a producer (*Witness*), originally went west from New York to become second in command to Kenny Hyman, who was then running Warner Bros. At a farewell dinner in New York, Feldman referred to his former boss Joseph E. Levine, who first made his mark distributing exploitation pictures like *Hercules.*

"The secret of Levine's success," Feldman told the gathering, "is that he underwent successful surgery to have his taste buds removed."

Of the current breed of Hollywood producers, I think of Sidney Beckerman as one of the more colorful. He once received the following cable from a friend in Monte Carlo.

HAVE BEEN IN TERRIBLE AUTOMOBILE AC-
CIDENT. LEG BEING AMPUTATED. DESPER-
ATELY NEED $15,000 TO COVER SURGERY
AND HOSPITALIZATION. PLEASE SEND.

Very familiar with his friend's gam-
bling proclivities, the suspicious Beckerman cabled back the following

IF YOU SEND LEG I'LL SEND MONEY.

Mike Todd, the producer of *Around
the World in 80 Days,* was one of the
movie world's most flamboyant and colorful producers. I wish I had known him.
While preparing a production of *War and
Peace* for filming in Yugoslavia, Todd, a
virtuoso promoter, actually talked Mar-
shal Tito, the head of state, into lending
him a division of the Yugoslavian army for
an entire month.

"Isn't that amazing?" commented one
very impressed Hollywood producer to
another.

"It'll be even more amazing if Tito
gets the division back."

○ 129 ○

Movies in general are very, very difficult to make. A good movie is a minor miracle, far harder to achieve, in my opinion, than a good play. You always start out to make it good, of course. No one, after all, ever took a script and said, "Oh, this is terrible. Let's shoot it." The intentions are always the best, but most of the work you do turns out to be poor. One of the things that make movies such a terribly difficult form is that for a variety of reasons, mostly having to do with things like the availability of actors and whether the scene is an interior or an exterior, they're shot in bits and pieces, and almost always out of sequence. Alfred Hitchcock once said to me, "It takes a lot of brains to make a bad movie." It isn't until you've shot your last scene that you can put all the fragments together, take a look, and get any sense of the overall. In the theater, from the very first day, the director can have the cast read through a play from beginning to end and get some sense of what they've got. In the movies all you can do at the end of each day is look at the previous day's rushes, which almost always look good. If they don't, you reshoot them. It's like the story about the pharaoh's daughter who finds a baby on the riverbank and brings him home to show her father.

"Isn't he beautiful?"

"Beautiful? I think he's ugly."

"I don't know," said the pharaoh's daughter, "he looked awfully good in the rushes."

There's usually a wrap party when the filming of a picture finally comes to an end. At the wrap party on *Bye Bye Birdie,* everyone, starting with the director, George Sidney, stood up and sang the praises of Ann-Margret, "the most talented," "the nicest," "the most beautiful," "the most adorable." On and on they went. Many toasts later, the last to rise was my dear friend Maureen Stapleton, who played Dick Van Dyke's mother.

"Well," she began, raising her glass somewhat shakily, "I guess I'm the only one on the picture who didn't want to fuck Ann-Margret."

When the shooting stops, the rough-cut screenings begin. Jack Lemmon asked his pal Walter Matthau to look at a rough cut of a picture he had just finished and about which he had some very serious doubts.

"What do you think?" asked Lemmon as the screening ended.

After a few thoughtful and suspense-filled moments, Matthau said, "Get out of it!"

Sidney Lumet invited about ten of his close friends to a rough-cut screening of *Prince of the City*. Like most directors, Sidney wanted some constructive suggestions at this early stage of the editing process. One of the invited, a notorious social opportunist, was more than a half hour late. Lumet, exasperated, said, "Where the hell is he?"

"Maybe," suggested Herb Sargent, a screen and TV writer, "he was invited to a rougher cut."

After watching several hours of assembled, unedited footage from *The Man of La Mancha,* the musical version of Cervantes's *Don Quixote,* a production executive at the financing company, United Artists, sensed an impending disaster. He slammed down his fist in the dark screening room and roared, "Eight million dollars for a picture and they couldn't even get Sancho Panza a decent horse?"

When the editing is finished, the sneak previews begin.

Dore Schary, the head of production at MGM, personally produced *The Next Voice You Hear,* a rather pretentious picture, I thought, in which the voice of God interrupts radio broadcasts with inspirational messages. One of its stars was Nancy Davis, a young actress who became Mrs. Ronald Reagan. It was obvious to all, after the first sneak preview, that the film was destined to be a financial disaster.

"One more picture like that," a junior executive at MGM was overheard saying to another, "and God will be out on his ass."

We sneaked *Let's Make Love*, the picture I made with Marilyn Monroe, in Reno as a convenience to Marilyn, who was shooting *The Misfits* nearby. Unfortunately, the sneak had to be canceled because there were devastating forest fires raging all around the area that day. "It's just as well," the picture's publicity man commented, "because Marilyn wasn't going to show up anyway."

After the sneak previews the picture finally opens, in the good old days at a premiere with klieg lights and Hollywood stars and celebrities. A valet parking attendant was reminded by his boss to pronounce Deborah Kerr's name properly when he announced over the public address system that her car had arrived.

"Car. Remember that her name rhymes with car. It's not Kerr as in fur."

The attendant said it over and over again to himself and when the time came he announced it perfectly.

"Deborah Kerr, your car is ready."

He sighed with relief. When the next car drove up in front of the theater, he made the following announcement:

"Alfred Hitchcar, your cock is ready."

The day of reckoning finally comes when the picture opens and it's reviewed. And, in Hollywood, you're only as good as your last picture. Walter Matthau and his wife, Carol, were reading the painfully bad notices of his latest starring vehicle.

"The worst part of it," Matthau remarked, "is now I'll have to start being nice to people again."

Hits are the extreme exception rather than the rule. There aren't nearly enough of them to go around, or so it often seems. Consequently, when a hit comes to someone else, it is often begrudged. For the lucky few the prevailing sentiment is "It's not enough that I succeed," as a true wit* once expressed it, "but all my friends

*La Rochefoucauld/Oscar Wilde/Ferenc Molnár/George Bernard Shaw/George S. Kaufman/William Lyon Phelps/Fred Allen/Oscar Levant/et cetera.

must fail." Billy Wilder said that there is
nothing that unifies the Hollywood community as much as a Peter Bogdanovich
failure.

Hollywood has always served the nation
well in wartime. Entertaining the boys in
uniform is a show biz tradition. Marilyn
Maxwell, the blond bombshell who was
once married to Jerry Davis, our producer
on *The Odd Couple,* was off in Korea with
Bob Hope during the Christmas season. A
short member of the troupe, whom we
shall call Rob, developed a great lust for
Maxwell, a Junoesque beauty. She would
simply push him away as you would a
naughty child.

"Rob," she'd say, "I'll let you know
when."

On this particular day, they finished
their show up in Panmunjom and were
flying back to Seoul in a two-engine trans-
port plane with bucket seats. They were
all cold, exhausted, and half asleep. Suddenly one of the engines conked out. Ev-

erybody woke up abruptly. Maxwell said, "Now, Rob."

During World War II, Artie Shaw, the bandleader, enlisted in the Navy and served in the Pacific, where he and his band performed for their fellow servicemen.

Harry Ruby, the songwriter, heard that Shaw was quoted as saying that he "couldn't wait to come to grips with the enemy."

"The closest Artie will ever come to the enemy," Ruby said, "is the lead sheet of 'Japanese Sandman.' "

There was a large and very interesting colony of European refugees, mostly Germans, who lived in Hollywood during the Second World War. Among them were such notables as the Nobel prize–winning author Thomas Mann and the German playwright Bertolt Brecht.

Otto Preminger, Viennese by birth, Prussian by temperament, grew increasingly impatient with a group of Hungarian refugees at the Players' Club because they were speaking to each other in their native language, not one word of which Preminger understood.

"God damn it," Preminger yelled at them, "we're in America now. Speak German like everybody else!"

Hollywood

abroad

.

"You want to go on location for a lousy desert scene? You gotta be kidding," said the studio's cost-conscious executive in charge of production to the director. "Shoot it in a sandtrap at the Hillcrest Country Club!"*

*B*Y THE TIME I got to Hollywood, not only were the golden days gone forever but the entire way of making movies had changed. Postwar audiences had become much more sophisticated and hungered for actual locales, as exotic and foreign as possible. And the influence of the Italian neorealist directors on their American counterparts was profound. Movies with that all-too-familiar look of studio back lots had become a thing of the past. Movies now had to be made on locations where the stories being told actually took place. Whether going on location is better or even necessary is an open question. At this writing I have just returned from endless weeks of shooting in Spain. There isn't a shot in the picture that couldn't have been made within fifty miles of Hollywood.

Before the war the New York locations of *Oh Men! Oh Women!* would've been shot either at the studio with us standing in front of a screen with shots of New York on it—rear projection, as it's called—or in New York by what's known as a second unit with other actors in long shots doubling for us. The days of shooting *How Green Was My Valley,* as an example, on the back lot of Fox in Beverly Hills had passed. That back lot is now Century City.

During the fifties and sixties many Hollywood movies were made abroad and Mike and I worked on our share of them. Overseas production was not entirely creatively motivated. The overriding incentive was financial: individual and corporate tax benefits, and the utilization of vast amounts of blocked foreign currencies accumulated by American businesses. Motion-picture production—the personnel in front of the cameras and behind them, the locations, the soundstages—became truly international and most of it was initiated, financed, and controlled by Hollywood's major studios.

Mervyn LeRoy, the American producer-director, was making *Quo Vadis* at Rome's Cinecittà Studio. Peter Ustinov, one of the picture's stars, invited a White Russian friend who lived in Rome to come to the studio. The mischievous actor introduced him to LeRoy, a militant, outspoken anticommunist, as the air attaché of the Soviet embassy in Rome. LeRoy had all he could do to be civil to the man.

When the Russian left the studio, LeRoy, puffing nervously on his cigar, asked Ustinov if the Soviets actually had an embassy in Rome.

"Of course they do," Ustinov replied, "just as the United States does."

"Yeah," said LeRoy, "but we got 'em all over the world!"

Of all the producers who worked abroad, Sam Spiegel was not only the most important and successful, but, it seems to me, the most colorful by far. The stories of his Byzantine, middle-European mind have always fascinated me—in part, I imagine, because it is so unlike my own.

Spiegel had left his homeland, Nazi Germany, with Otto Preminger. As their train approached the Dutch border, Preminger, wise to the ways of his lifelong friend, cautioned Spiegel.

"This is not the time for any of your nonsense, Sam. Our lives are at stake."

"Do you think I'm crazy?"

German border guards entered their compartment, checked their papers, and asked if they were carrying any contraband—German currency, jewels, and so on.

"Absolutely not," they both replied.

As the train crossed the border into Holland and, at long last, they were safe, Spiegel reached into an inside pocket of

Preminger's overcoat, which was hanging from a hook, and removed a huge roll of German marks. Preminger was aghast.

"I didn't tell you," Spiegel said calmly, "because I thought it might make you nervous."

When Spiegel and the director David Lean were preparing *Lawrence of Arabia* for production, they needed King Hussein's permission to shoot certain key sequences in the Kingdom of Jordan. An exceedingly generous and gracious host, Spiegel invited Hussein to join him on his luxurious yacht, which was anchored in the Mediterranean off Cannes. During conversation, the king made a reference to Ramadan.

"What's Ramadan?" Spiegel asked.

"That," the king explained, "is the Islamic religion's holy month."

"Ah, yes," said Spiegel, doing his absolute utmost to make his leonine head look its most Roman, "that's like our Lent."

The king, by the way, granted Spiegel permission to film in Jordan and Hussein subsequently married a young English-woman who worked on *Lawrence* as a production secretary. Unfortunately, she was killed several years later in a helicop-ter crash.

Spiegel was preparing a picture in London with Robert Parrish, the director, and they were having a lot of problems with the script.

"There's only one man who can help us lick this," said Parrish.

"Who's that?"

"Billy Wilder."

Spiegel, a man of action, got on the phone with Wilder, whom his secretary had tracked down in Switzerland, and ex-plained the problem.

"I'll tell you what, Sam," Wilder said, "I'll give you a free week if you can get me the royal suite at the Hôtel de Paris in Monte Carlo for two weeks."

The dates Wilder wanted were at the height of the tourist season.

"I've tried everyone I know," he went on, "and no one has been able to help me."

"Okay," Spiegel said, "it's a deal."

Spiegel got off the phone and resumed the story conference with Parrish. After fifteen minutes had gone by, he called Wilder again.

"Okay, Billy, you're all set. You've got the suite. Now, when can you get to London to work with us?"

Spiegel spent most of the next week pulling every string he had to get the accommodations. Eventually he did. But in the meantime he had left Wilder with the impression that it had taken him no longer than fifteen minutes to accomplish the impossible.

Robert Bolt, a painstakingly slow craftsman, was writing the screenplay for *Lawrence of Arabia* when he was arrested in London at an antinuke demonstration. He called Spiegel from jail.

"Sam, get me out of here."

"Give me ten pages and I'll do it."

Spiegel announced to the press that the best-selling novel *The Night of the Generals* was going to be his next picture.

He told his publicity man, Arthur Cantor, that Anatole Litvak would be directing it.

"But, Sam, you need a young director for that picture."

"No, I want Litvak. He's perfect for it."

"Why?"

"Because he owns the book."

The only motion-picture producer I know of with a mind almost as convoluted as Spiegel's was Raoul Lévy, the Frenchman who made many of Brigitte Bardot's films, starting with her first, *And God Created Woman.* Most of the movies Lévy made were financed by Columbia Pictures. He, like Spiegel, was accomplished in a half a dozen languages. His eighty-five-foot yacht, the *Babette,* wasn't nearly as big as Spiegel's, which was a converted Canadian minesweeper, but he enjoyed himself nonetheless cruising the Mediterranean.

Lévy actually said to a bewildered vice-president of Van Cleef & Arpels jewelers in New York, an establishment to which he then owed $95,000, "Listen, if it weren't for people like me who owed you a lot of money, you'd be out of business.''

Mike once asked him how he could stand owing such enormous sums of money. "Don't you have trouble sleeping?''

"Don't be silly,'' Lévy replied. "The people I owe all the money to aren't sleeping, so why should I be losing sleep as well?''

One day Alain Bernheim, a producer who was then an agent, knowing that Lévy was broke, invited him to lunch at one of Paris's most expensive restaurants. As they were leaving Bernheim's office, Raoul borrowed 100 francs (about $20) from the switchboard operator.

"What's that for?'' Bernheim asked.

"To tip the maître d'.''

Never exactly the soul of discretion, Lévy was checking into the Connaught, London's most elegant and exclusive hotel, with Jeanne Moreau. When they were given rooms several floors apart, he said to the very proper and formal manager, Mr. Gustav, in a voice that resounded through the lobby, "What the hell do you want me to do, take the elevator and walk through the halls in my pajamas?"

Lévy was convinced that *Moderato Cantabile,* his production starring Jeanne Moreau and Jean-Paul Belmondo, written by Marguerite Duras, directed by Peter Brook, and financed by Columbia, would win the Palme d'or at that year's Cannes Film Festival. Despite its impressive credentials, the picture turned out to be a tedious, endless bore in which Moreau and Belmondo never stopped talking and walking.

"Well, maybe it won't win the Festival," the resilient Lévy said after further consideration, "but it would have a hell of a chance in the Boston Marathon."

Lévy had his ups and downs, financially and emotionally. He eventually took his own life at the age of forty-four on New Year's Eve 1966 in Saint-Tropez with a shotgun he had rented. It seems to me it may have been the only practical thing the customarily extravagant Lévy ever did.

Before Jack Clayton became a direc-

tor (*Room at the Top, The Pumpkin Eater*),
he was an eager and ambitious young production manager. He was in his office on
the Tyrrhenian coast when Jimmy Wolf,
the producer of *Beat the Devil,* called on
the ship-to-shore phone to say that Jennifer Jones and John Huston, the director,
had had a dispute and that she had left
the freighter, on which most of the picture was being filmed, and was heading
back to shore. Clayton was instructed to
use whatever means he had at his command to prevail on the star to return to
the ship, which was about ten miles off
the Italian coast. If he failed, an entire
day's shooting would be lost.

Clayton paced the dock, eagerly
awaiting Jones. When she arrived in a motor launch, he turned his considerable
charm on her. She relented after a while
and the two of them returned to the ship.
Triumphant, Clayton entered Huston's
cabin.

"She's here," Clayton said.

"Who's here?" Huston asked.

"Jennifer."

"Jennifer!" Huston bellowed. "If you don't get that cunt off this ship . . ."

When Joe Mankiewicz decided to leave Hollywood and go out on his own, he made most of his subsequent pictures abroad—*The Barefoot Contessa, The Quiet American, Suddenly Last Summer, Cleopatra, Sleuth.* They did relatively better at the box office in European countries than in the States. Mankiewicz once said, "I think they gain something in the translation." When he was staging the most spectacular and expensive scene in *Cleopatra*—the Egyptian queen's procession into ancient Rome—everything had to be planned and meticulously prepared down to the smallest detail: thousands of elaborately costumed extras, exquisitely caparisoned elephants, zebras, and a variety of other exotic creatures, many of which had been painted in a variety of unusual patterns and hues. At the center of it all was Elizabeth Taylor, looking her most ravishing, seated on her royal palanquin, borne by a retinue of Nubian slaves. A battery of cameras was poised at the

1

Except for *The Odd Couple*, this is the longest run I've ever had: four years in the U.S. Army.
Rembrandt Studio

2

My first show on Broadway, *Antony and Cleopatra*, William Shakespeare's play about Scarus, a messenger, who brings tidings of the historic battle of Actium. I, of course, played Scarus. That's Katharine Cornell whose hand I'm kissing and Godfrey Tearle. I can't imagine what I was doing with my left hand.

3

After my triumph in Shakespeare, I went on to do Bernard Shaw's play about an Egyptian majordomo in which I was supported by Sir Cedric Hardwicke and Lilli Palmer as Caesar and Cleopatra.

The Theatre Collection, Museum of the City of New York

Randall, Tony **LExington 2-1100**
TELEPHONE EXCHANGE

Height _____ 5'11" Hair _____ Brown
Weight _____ 160 Eyes _____ Brown

LEADS - CHARACTER - JUVENILE - ANNOUNCER

RADIO: "Reggie" on I Love a Mystery, Mr. District Attorney, Perry Mason, Henry Morgan Show, etc., etc.

STAGE: Barretts of Wimpole Street, Anthony and Cleopatra with Cornell, Caesar and Cleopatra, To Tell You the Truth, etc., etc.

T.V. Mac, the sailor, on One Man's Family, Philco, etc., etc.

4

My all-important "Lex" card, which is what we thespians left at the offices of producers, casting agents, etc., when we made the rounds. Lexington is how they reached us in the days before answering machines. If the message was really important, Lex tracked us down, no matter where.

5

Wally Cox appears to be unhappy, but the chances are the rest of us—Marion Lorne (sitting in front), Pat Benoit, and I—were laughing at something funny he had just said.

6

Paul Muni is the cynosure of (from left to right) Ed Begley, *moi*, and Louis Hector in the Broadway production of *Inherit the Wind*. Muni had the greatest stage voice I have ever heard and his acting was so fascinating that often I was pulled out of my role in the play into the role of a fan.

*The Theatre Collection, Museum
of the City of New York*

Oh Men! Oh Women!—my first movie. David Niven is standing so stiffly beside Dan Dailey because he was suffering back spasms. He couldn't move and so for two or three days we did something that can't be done in the theater: we shot around him.

8

Pillow Talk is the first picture I made with Rock Hudson and Doris Day. "And," I'm telling them, "if I don't get to do at least two more pictures with you, I'm walking." And so we made *Lover Come Back* and *Send Me No Flowers* together.

ready to film the scene from every conceivable angle.

The heat that day in Rome on the back lot at Cinecittà was intense. At long last, after endless exhausting hours, everything was exactly as Mankiewicz wanted it. The moment had finally come.

"Action!" Mankiewicz said through his bullhorn.

The procession began. The cameras turned. And then, quite suddenly and unexpectedly, Mankiewicz yelled, "Cut!" The procession ground to a halt.

Why?

Because in the middle of everything Mankiewicz spotted a very enterprising Italian ice-cream vendor hawking his refreshing wares. "Gelati! Gelati!" he was shouting. And, what's more, some of the extras were buying.

One afternoon Mike visited the set of *Cleopatra*. He was on crutches and his left leg was in a cast up to his crotch. He had broken it very badly in a skiing accident in Switzerland several months before. Mankiewicz, who hadn't seen Mike since they had worked together on *The Quiet American* in Saigon and Rome, crossed the soundstage and looked him over very slowly and deliberately. "You know," Mankiewicz said, finally breaking the silence, "I could write you out of that."

Fireworks were needed for a scene in *The Quiet American,* which Mankiewicz was filming in Vietnam. He was taken on a tour of a fireworks factory on the outskirts of Saigon where, to his astonishment, he saw that many of the workers were smoking.

"I understand," said Mankiewicz to the factory foreman, "that there was a terrible explosion here last year and that several workers were killed."

"Oh," the Vietnamese replied sadly, "every year."

Just before filming started on *The Quiet American,* the Vietnamese government gave a reception to welcome the company to Saigon. Mike was introduced to a Miss Phuc, whom he took by the hand and brought across the room to Mankiewicz.

"Joe, I want you to meet Miss Phuc."

"Oh," said Mankiewicz as he shook her hand, "what year?"

One of the disadvantages of shooting films so far from Hollywood, as I understand it, is that the studios find it far more difficult to exercise their customarily rigid fiscal controls. *What's New, Pussycat?* was behind schedule and alarmingly over budget, mostly because of its star, Peter Sellers, who was being his most difficult and temperamental. Growing increasingly concerned, United Artists dispatched its ace troubleshooter to London to get things under control. He flew all night, checked into the Dorchester Hotel, dragged himself to the elevator, and there was Woody Allen, the film's author and costar.

"Hiya, Woody."

"What are you doing in town?"

"I've come to straighten everything out," the executive replied. "I'm going to read the riot act to that horse's ass Peter Sellers and put an end to his nonsense once and for all."

The elevator stopped; Allen exited

and walked past another man in black horn-rimmed glasses.

"Good morning, Woody," said the man leaving the elevator.

"Hiya, Peter," said the man entering the elevator.

Oh, my God! realized the executive. *That wasn't Woody Allen I was speaking to, that was Peter Sellers!*—whose genius for mimicry included the most convincing American accent by a Britisher I have ever heard, even better than Peter Ustinov's.

The production fell behind even farther, for after that encounter with UA's troubleshooter in the Dorchester elevator, Sellers disappeared for three days.

There were sizable colonies of Americans living in the film capitals of the world, especially in London, during the period when motion-picture production was flourishing abroad. Some—men like Joe Losey, Carl Foreman, and Sidney Buchman—were refugees from Hollywood's infamous blacklist. There were, in fact, so many Americans living in London that they started a regular softball game on Sundays in Hyde Park. It was immortalized in the movie *A Touch of Class*, starring George Segal. Among the regulars were the founders of the game—Norman Panama and his partner Mel Frank, who directed and cowrote *A Touch of Class*, Harvey Orkin, the agent, John Kohn, the American writer-producer *(The Collector)*, Kenny Hyman, the producer of *The Dirty Dozen*, and Mike. Elliott Gould, Jim Brown, the great football player who was acting in *The Dirty Dozen*, Tony Curtis, and any other visiting Americans who happened to be in London joined the game. Stephanie Powers led the cheering section and Ingrid Boulting and Samantha Eggar looked on in bewilderment at the confounding American game. For a while the game was moved to the playground of a church in Chelsea until one Sunday when there was a notice on the bulletin board that read, "It's all right for the Americans to bring their sticks but they will have to leave their balls at home." Back to Hyde Park they went.

Arthur Lewis, a producer who was one of the game's regulars, actually made it to the big leagues. His boyhood friend, Joe L. Brown, Jr., the general manager of the Pittsburgh Pirates, invited him to join the team for spring training in Florida and Lewis jumped at the opportunity to fulfill a lifelong fantasy. They gave Arthur his own uniform and to all intents and purposes he became a member of the team, participating in all of its activities—fielding practice, pepper drills, calisthenics, and last—but very far from least—batting practice. A dream of glory! Before stepping into the batter's box for the first time, Lewis, his heart pounding, his hands shaking, tugged at the bill of his cap and knocked the dirt out of his spikes with his bat, the way the pros do. And right then and there his spring training came to an abrupt end. Lewis's bat missed his spikes and broke his ankle.

During my working visits to London I spent time with quite a few of these expatriates.

Marsha, the wife of Norman Panama,

the writer-director with Mel Frank of so many of the Bob Hope pictures—was shopping one morning, well into the sixties, and it was taking longer than usual to get waited on in her neighborhood butcher shop. Contrary to all of our expectations about Anglo-Saxon cultures, England is very far from the most efficient of societies. Growing increasingly impatient, she complained.

"But, Mrs. Panama," the butcher responded, "you must understand that we've been very shorthanded since the war."

Burt Shevelove, a very original and beloved man, directed Broadway shows (*A Funny Thing Happened on the Way to the Forum*), as well as industrial shows and a lot of television, which is how I knew him. He became an expatriate in the seventies, later than most Americans. When he wasn't using his flat in London's West End, he was very generous about offering it to visiting friends.

He let Herb Sargent, the writer, use it when he was in London on a brief working visit. "Don't thank me, Herb, just leave a little something under my pillow."

Shevelove's wonderful collection of books and memorabilia filled every room. His collection of grotesqueries—pictures, drawings, posters, and paintings of freaks, monsters, mutants, dwarfs, giants, elephant men, bearded ladies, dog-faced boys, deformed and defective animals and humans—adorned the walls in the bedroom of his flat where I and many others were frequent recipients of his hospitality.

Sargent asked Shevelove how he could open his eyes every day to that display.

"Honey," Shevelove, not a handsome man, responded, "when I wake up in the morning, I want to know I'm the prettiest thing in that room."

Shevelove died in London and his niece, Judith Levin, flew back to New York with his ashes, which the funeral home had placed in an ugly plastic container. Just before his funny and moving memorial service, which filled the Booth Theatre, his niece called one of Burt's closest friends, Mary Rodgers, the composer Richard's daughter, and said, "I think the time has come to decant Burt."

When they got drunk enough, the two of them—'twixt the tears and laughter—poured their beloved Burt's ashes from the plastic container into a beautiful antique box, which they were certain he, a man of impeccable taste, would prefer.

Larry Gelbart, who lived in London for quite a long time, and Alain Bernheim had a project they wanted to speak to Lord Snowden about. An appointment was made for them at Clarence House, where the earl and Princess Margaret resided. The meeting took place in one of the palace's rooms in which Anthony Armstrong-Jones, as he was known professionally, kept an enormous amount of highly sophisticated radio and electronic equipment.

"Your Highness," Gelbart asked, "can you get the BBC on that?"

Larry and I worked together on a television show at ITV, one of England's commercial networks. "The English," said Larry to me one day as we were lunching in the cafeteria, "they're twenty-five years ahead of us in bad food."

Larry Adler, the American harmonica virtuoso, was an involuntary expatriate, a political exile living in London because he was blacklisted in the States. During the Korean War, Larry went to Japan to entertain the British troops. While there, he went to watch the great Japanese director Akira Kurosawa film a scene on location outside Tokyo. Adler waited for several hours, but not a single foot of film was exposed.

"I wait for crowd," Kurosawa explained.

Adler stayed awhile longer and then told the director that he had to leave because he was giving a concert for the troops in Tokyo later that day.

"But please explain something to me. Doesn't it cost a lot of money to sit around like this without doing anything? Why don't you arrange beforehand to have the crowd come?"

"Oh," Kurosawa said, pointing to the sky, "you don't understand. I wait for crowd to pass sun."

Sir Basil Spence, the renowned English architect who had supervised the restoration of the bombed-out Coventry Cathedral, was invited to spend some time at Shepperton Studio with John Bryan, the gifted art director who designed the interior of historic Canterbury Cathedral for the motion picture *Becket.* Bryan took Spence on a tour of the scenery and property shops, where he watched the master craftsmen at work. They then went to look at the various sets on the soundstages. Like everyone else I have ever seen who visits a movie studio for the first time, Spence was overwhelmed by the magic of it all. Their day together ended in a screening room where they looked at a pivotal scene in the cathedral. They sat in rapt silence watching the picture's stars, Richard Burton and Peter O'Toole, perform. Spence, the architect, was unable to contain his enthusiasm any longer. "Oh," he exclaimed, "that's perfect! Perfect! The walls are absolutely perfect!"

Paris was also a center of American film-making activity in those days. For a while there was even a softball game in the Bois de Boulogne.

Irwin Shaw, one of the most famous of all American expatriates, and the director Robert Parrish had still not found a leading man to play opposite Jean Seberg in their picture *In the French Style,* and they were only a week away from their start date. Irwin, the writer and producer of the picture, was drinking late one night at his usual table in the Relais of the Plaza-Athénée Hotel, when he spotted Lou Cioffi, ABC-TV's Paris correspondent. My God, thought Shaw, Lou's the perfect guy for it—handsome, worldly, and he's certainly got to be comfortable in front of a camera.

"Lou, how would you like to be a movie star?"

Cioffi couldn't resist. The possibility of becoming a movie star, I have found, intrigues everyone. Two days later Cioffi was on a soundstage at the Billancourt Studio with Jean Seberg, Robert Parrish, the director, and Shaw.

Everything went extremely well during the rehearsal. It looked as if Shaw's inspiration was going to pay off. At a certain point in the scene, Cioffi was directed to rise, pat Jean on the top of her blond head with his right hand as he said his lines, and then exit. Otherwise, the entire scene was to be played with the two of them seated at a table. What could be easier?

"Okay, let's try one," said Parrish, as every director I have ever worked with says every time.

As soon as Parrish called out, "Action," Cioffi froze. His eyes bugged, his brow sweated. With his hands clasped tightly together he recited Shaw's lines like an automaton. When he rose to pat Jean on her head, he did it with both hands because his fingers were intertwined so tightly that he couldn't pull them apart!

It was hopeless. They didn't even bother to get the film processed at the laboratory. Afterward Parrish asked Shaw, never known for his tact or delicacy, just how he was going to let his friend Cioffi down gently.

"Don't worry, I'll find a way."

He got Cioffi on the phone. "Hello, Lou. It's Irwin. Forget it, kid—you can't act!"

English actor Stanley Baker got the part.

Mike had broken his leg skiing with Irwin Shaw in Switzerland—as had so many others, that Mike dubbed him "the Judas goat of the mountains," a shill for the local hospital. At a dinner party in Paris, a French literary critic told Shaw that he had been the first in France to review his novel *The Young Lions* and that although he thought Shaw was an "old whore," he admired the book enormously. Without saying anything Shaw turned away from the man, hesitated, turned back, and punched him right in the jaw. Author raps critic. Now, that's what I call a role reversal! "I'm sick and tired," Shaw explained to the gathering later, "of people who think they have the right to say anything they please to me." It is a sentiment, I must say, all of us in the business share.

"Get him out of here," Shaw screamed.

It looked as though he might hit the man again and so Mike got up—his left leg still in a metal brace—and threw his arms around Shaw, who was about twice Mike's size. As Shaw tried his best to shake him off, Mike dangled from him, as if from a great bear. Alain Bernheim, their host, came to Mike's rescue and the two of them managed to push Irwin back over the arm of a sofa and onto the seat cushions. Shaw continued to scream imprecations as they sat on him. When he quieted down they let him up. But he saw that the critic was still there and his anger flared again.

"Get him out of here, God damn it!"

Marian, his beautiful wife, came up to him. With Alain and Mike on either side holding his arms down, she stood directly in front of Shaw, grabbed his earlobes, looked him in the eyes, and in a very calm, deliberate, penetrating voice said, "Whatever it is you're doing, stop it. Do you hear me, Irwin? Stop it!"

This seemed to have a very calming effect on Irwin until the woman who had introduced him to the critic came over to apologize.

"God damn it," Irwin yelled at her, "it's your fault for introducing us!"

Shaw broke Bernheim's grip and sent the woman sprawling across the living room with one swipe of his huge forearm. She ended up on the floor, beneath the piano, crying hysterically. Alain's mother then came up to Irwin with a glass of water in her left hand. She dipped a few fingers of her right hand into the glass and flicked the cold water into Irwin's face several times. What a scene!

They finally got the critic to leave and things at the party returned to normal. Later in the evening, as Mike and his wife, Freda, were leaving, Irwin said to him,

"This won't get into the papers, will it?" Since Gene Moscowitz, *Variety*'s Paris correspondent, was the only journalist present, Mike told Irwin he thought it was highly unlikely because *Variety*, the show-business bible, did not have a sports page.

They're still playing baseball in Hyde Park on Sundays, but it's not the same. The teams now consist mostly of Americans in the business community. Almost all of the game's originals have returned to the States as Hollywood's participation in European motion-picture production has come to a virtual halt. What a shame. It certainly gave birth to a lot of wonderful times and stories—and some damn good pictures too.

6

Hollywood

anonymous

---○---

"I'm going to tell you a delicious piece of gossip," said Hans Habe, the German writer, to a group of his friends. "Now, listen very carefully because I'm only going to tell it once because I promised not to repeat it!"

---○---

*I*N THIS, the briefest of all my chapters, I am willing, to a limited extent, to indulge the reader's lust for gossip by recounting several of the more wicked Hollywood tales. Almost all, for obvious reasons, are not for attribution. A few are for attribution in part.

Reader, let your imagination chew on what meager clues I provide.

A famous writer-director was describing a renowned producer, both of whom I have mentioned previously. How's that for tantalizing?

"He's great in an emergency. Let's say you were a married man and you were shacked up in some motel with a whore and she died. He's the guy you'd call. He'd come right over and take care of every-thing—get rid of the body—you name it. But first, of course, he'd screw her."

The president of one of Hollywood's unions—creative, not craft—was involved in a particularly acrimonious and divisive negotiation with the studios. The leader of a rival faction within the union said of the president, long noted for the obvious hairpiece he wears, "When this is all over, I'd like to pull the rug right out from over him."

There was a script editor who worked regularly in Hollywood for years. Once a week he visited a prostitute who performed an erotic dance and then took him to bed. The charge was $25. After about ten years she informed him that she was raising her price to $35. It came as a blow because he was very tight with a buck.

"I know," he said after giving it some very careful thought, "let's cut the dance."

One of Hollywood's more celebrated wits went to hear the wife of a close friend sing in a nightclub. His friend worked the lights during the song session and led the applause after each number.

"Love," the wit commented after the show, "is also deaf."

From time to time the wife of an important Hollywood personality works on pictures as an extra. When the assistant director of *Airport* placed her in the economy section of the mock-up plane on a soundstage at Universal, she insisted on being seated in first class.

Men, as we sometimes do, sit around and swap notes about women. On this particular evening there were about ten men and the subject was the best lover they had ever had. It was Warren Beatty's turn and he told the gathering that of all the women he'd made love to, the best, without question, was his current flame, a Hollywood star. "It's not because I'm going with her now. She just happens to be far and away the best I've ever had." A few turns later a Hollywood writer simply said, "I have to agree with Warren."

A Hollywood producer was driving home after a night on the town with the boys. He was drunk. Within a few blocks of his home two California Highway patrolmen pulled up behind him and ordered him out of his car. He was trying to walk a straight line when the police heard the nearby sound of a terrible car crash. They told the producer to wait as they ran back and around a bend in the road toward the source of the sound. The producer drove home, put the car in his garage, ran, as best he could, into the house, and told his wife that if the police came she was to say that he was in bed and had been home all night.

A little while later the police arrived. Where, they asked the producer's wife, was her husband? "In bed. He's been home all night."

"And where is his car?"

"In the garage."

"Open it, please."

And she did. And there, inside the garage, was the police car.

Doris LeRoy Vidor, Harry Warner's daughter, gave a dinner party at which a famous Hollywood writer-director and her other guests listened to a fascinating story told by a European woman whom no one there but the hostess had ever met before. A few years later a motion picture, obviously based on that story, was released. Doris called her friend, the writer-director, to say how delighted she was that he had been able to use the story he had heard at her dinner party.

"What story?"

Sometime after that, the writer-director called Doris to say that he was being sued by another writer for plagiarism.

Would Doris be willing to testify that he had, in fact, heard the story one evening at her dinner party?

"What dinner party?" she responded.

7

Where would we be without them?

---○---

The dinner parties at the producer Arthur Hornblow's house were among Hollywood's most elegant. One evening Herman Mankiewicz, who co-wrote with Orson Welles Citizen Kane, *generally regarded as the best screenplay ever written, drank so much that in the middle of the meal he suddenly became ill, bent over, and threw up. The host and his then wife, Myrna Loy, and all their guests were aghast.*

"It's all right, Arthur," Mankiewicz reassured his host as he surfaced from beneath the table, "the white wine came up with the fish."

---○---

I N THE THEATER, as in the Bible, everything begins with the word. "If it ain't on the page, it ain't on the stage," goes the old theatrical saying. The acting, the direction, the sets and costumes, can all bedazzle, but if the words aren't right, then nothing else matters. In the theater, as is not the case in films, a play cannot be changed in the least particular without the playwright's consent, thanks to the rights gained over the years by the Dramatists' Guild.

Writing for the theater is, it seems to me, the most difficult and demanding of all. And it is often the least rewarding financially. Stage actresses interested in security are much better off with stagehands, who day in and day out are the best paid people in the theater.

The French playwright Tristan Bernard kept his hard-earned royalty money in a French bank that was protected by an imposing, resplendently uniformed, rifle-bearing guard. When the playwright fell on hard times, he withdrew the last of his francs and closed the account. On his way out he walked over to the guard and said, with great panache, "So far as I'm concerned, you can go home now."

Oklahoma! became a hit after Oscar Hammerstein, the lyricist, had four successive flops. The week after *Oklahoma!*

opened on Broadway, Hammerstein, a humble man, took an ad in *Variety* listing his four previous flops. *"And,"* the ad concluded, *"I could do it again."*

Ferenc Molnár, the Hungarian playwright whose many wonderful works included *Liliom,* had a very up-and-down career. A sybarite, he always lived in the finest places in the world, among which, in those days, was the Plaza Hotel in New York. When he had a hit, he stayed in a magnificent suite and when he wasn't doing well he lived in a broom closet. Molnár had just had a hit play open on Broadway—maybe it was *The Guardsman* with the Lunts—and he was back on top of the world. He was on his way to Cartier's to buy a bauble for his latest flame, and Alexander Ince, a producer, magazine publisher, and fellow Hungarian, offered to go with him.

"What do I need you for?"

"Someday you'll be down on your luck again and broke," Ince said, "and then you'll know who your real friends are. I want you always to remember that I stuck by you when you had money."

Arthur Miller, our greatest living dramatist, is among the theater's most successful. He was making a sentimental journey back to his old neighborhood in Brooklyn. While walking past a sidewalk fruit-and-vegetable stand he heard someone call out, "Artie!" He turned and saw a man, about his age, standing with a white apron tied around his waist.

"Aren't you Artie Miller?"

"Yes."

"It's me, Mike. Mike Kelly," the man said, smiling. "We went to high school together."

"Well, for God's sake! Mike. Of course I remember. How are you?"

"Fine. Just fine. Tell me, Artie—what do you do now?"

"I'm a writer, Mike. I write plays, movies, an occasional book."

"Do you make a living?"

"A very good living."

"You know, maybe that's what I should've done."

Two of the English theater's most successful playwrights are Peter Shaffer *(The Royal Hunt of the Sun, Equus, Amadeus,* etc.) and his identical twin brother Tony *(Sleuth)*. One day Peter—or perhaps it was Tony—ran into someone he hadn't seen in quite a long time.

"I can never remember," said the acquaintance, "whether it was you or your brother who was killed in the war."

Hollywood frequently buys plays like *Equus,* and then spends a lot of time and effort trying to figure out how they can possibly be made into commercial movies. "That's easy," said Neil Simon of *Equus,* a play in which an emotionally disturbed stable boy blinds several horses. "They should use name horses."

When Neil was writing his first play, *Come Blow Your Horn,* his experience as a writer was limited to television comedy. Neil would take his pages to Reggie Rose every day that summer on Fire Island and they'd go over them together. When the play was finally finished, Neil asked Reggie how he could thank him. "Pass it on,"

Reggie replied. And Simon's been doing that one way or another ever since.

The ways of the creative unconscious are often mysterious. One of the biggest laughs in *The Odd Couple* comes when Oscar tells Felix that he can't stand finding those notes he's been leaving on his pillow in which he says things like *"We're out of cornflakes. F.U."* The huge laugh it got came as a complete surprise to Neil Simon at the play's first performance before an audience. Until then Neil hadn't realized that Unger, the surname he had given Felix with no thought of a joke, made his initials F.U.

Robert Sherwood, who was one of our theater's greatest playwrights, told me the following story, which he swore was absolutely untrue. Many years ago Sherwood ran into the producer Max Gordon walking down Broadway.

"Why do you have such a big smile on your face, Max?"

"Why shouldn't I be happy?" Gordon said. "I've got the biggest hit in town, and the star of the show"—let's call her Fifi

Bijou—"is the world's greatest cock-sucker."

Years passed and Robert Sherwood was walking through the Senate Office Building when he ran into Senator Estes Kefauver during the time of the hearings on organized crime. Kefauver had just finished interviewing Virginia Hill before her scheduled testimony in front of the TV cameras the following day.

"Now, Miss Hill," the senator said, "you own considerable property: in Beverly Hills you own a beautiful home, you have a car, you own other property in the South and you own another home in Hawaii, if I'm not mistaken, and yet you have no visible means of income. I must ask you, Miss Hill, what the source is of all these real goods?"

"Senator," Hill replied, "I'm the world's greatest cocksucker, and if you ask me that same question on live television tomorrow, that's the answer you're going to get."

Sherwood ran to the phone and sent the following telegram to his wife: FIFI BI-

JOU TITLE JUST PREEMPTED BY VIR-
GINIA HILL.

There was a Broadway producer who
wanted to do a revival of Samson Raphaelson's lovely play *Accent on Youth,* but I
couldn't come to terms with him. He was
under the impression that I liked the play
so much that I would do it for very little.
Sam, who was then about ninety-five,
called me up and said, "I just would love
to see a play of mine on Broadway again
before I die and I only have between ten
minutes and four years left." Unfortunately, although we came very close to a
deal, the producer and I had a falling out
and the play wasn't done. And soon after,
Sam Raphaelson died. The day after, I ran
into Hume Cronyn and told him the story.
"And," I said in conclusion, "I killed Sam
Raphaelson." To which Hume, who had
had a lot of unhappy experiences with
him in a play of his called *Jason,* responded, "Good!"

I can't talk about writers without
mentioning some of those gifted men and

women who write the melodies, lyrics, and librettos—the books, as they're known to us in the theater—for our musical theater.

Just who writes what is often confusing to the public. Mrs. Jerome Kern, the composer's widow, and Mrs. Oscar Hammerstein, the lyricist's widow, were at a party together when their hostess introduced them to another guest. "And," the hostess went on to explain, "Mrs. Kern's husband wrote 'Ol' Man River.'"

"No, no, her husband wrote 'dum, dum da dum,'" Mrs. Hammerstein interjected. *"My* husband wrote 'Ol' Man River.'"

Lyricist-librettist Betty Comden *(On the Town, Bells Are Ringing,* etc.) and her husband, Steve Kyle, were at an art gallery in Greenwich Village on a Saturday afternoon watching in amazement as an automated machine splashed paint on a canvas. The gallery owner asked them for their impression of the mechanical action artist.

"We have a three-year-old phonograph at home that can paint better than that," Kyle replied.

All of us, no matter how gifted, celebrated, and successful, need approval. Hal Prince, who went on to become one of Broadway's most successful directors and producers, was at the time of this story the young, eager second assistant stage manager of Irving Berlin's *Call Me Madam,* which was in rehearsal. The phone backstage rang and Prince picked it up.

"Hello, this is Irving Berlin. Is Leland Hayward there?"

Hayward was the musical's producer.

"No, sir."

"How about Ethel Merman?"—the show's star.

"No, sir."

"Then get me Howard Lindsay," the coauthor of the show's book.

"He's not here, sir."

"What about Russel Crouse?"—Lindsay's collaborator.

"He's not here either."

"Well," said Berlin, "who's this?"

"I'm Hal Prince, sir, the second assistant stage manager."

"I see. Tell me, Hal, what do you think of this?"

And over the telephone came the strains of Berlin singing and playing the song he had just finished writing: "I Hear Singing and There's No One There."

I'm quite certain that if it had been the cleaning woman who had picked up the phone, Berlin would've done the same thing. And he, it must be remembered, is the composer/lyricist of whom the great Jerome Kern, when asked what Berlin's place was in American music, remarked, "Berlin *is* American music."

Several years ago Neil Simon approached Berlin about using some of his songs in a musical he was contemplating.

"Not now," Berlin, who was then about ninety-five, replied. "Maybe in a few years."

I was doing a show up in Syracuse, New York, celebrating the hometown boy, Jimmy Van Heusen, one of the top songwriters in Hollywood. Forty-five big hits in a row were sung by the likes of Tony Bennett, Jack Jones, Maggie Whiting, Maxine Sullivan. It was just gigantic, one of the best shows I've ever seen or been a part of. Tony Bennett said to me, "What a show! Every number is better than the one that follows it!"

Andrew Lloyd Webber has composed some of the most successful musicals in the theater's history (*Cats, Phantom of the Opera,* etc.). When Webber and Alan Jay Lerner, the lyricist of *My Fair Lady, Brigadoon,* etc., were working together on a project, Webber asked his collaborator why so many people seemed to take an immediate dislike to him.

"To save time," Lerner responded.

Jule Styne, who ranks high on my list of composers (*Gypsy, Funny Girl, High Button Shoes, Bells Are Ringing,* etc.), was collaborating on a musical with Herb Gardner, the playwright, who had never worked on one before. Gardner came to him one day with pages of lyrics.

"What's that?" Jule asked.

"They're my lyrics for that song we talked about."

"All that's a lyric?" Styne said in astonishment. " 'I've flown around the world in a plane;/ I've settled revolutions in Spain;/ The North Pole I have charted,/ Still I can't get started with you.' That's a lyric. Case dismissed!"

Sammy Cahn, the lyricist who won an Academy Award with Jule for *Three Coins in the Fountain*, had a very unhappy first marriage. Very often when they were dinner guests at the homes of friends, Cahn would say to his wife, "Now, why don't we have food like this at our home?"

It became like a tic, embarrassing not only to his wife but to their friends as well.

One evening when Cahn said it once again—"Now, why can't we have food like this at our home?"—his wife replied, "But Sammy, this is our home."

Joe Stein, the librettist of *Fiddler on the Roof*, has a special knack for putting things in proper perspective. As he was boarding a flight to Los Angeles, he ran into Mike, who had read in that morning's *New York Times* that the movie rights to *Fiddler* had been sold for four million dollars.

"My God, Joe, what a lot of money!"

"Not really," Joe shrugged. "It's only about ten minutes in the Vietnam War."

Screenwriters, unlike playwrights, have no power and are accorded very little respect. In Hollywood, scripts are rewritten, more often than not, by a battery of writers, with little if any regard for the original author's intentions.

Don't Make Waves's sole distinction as a picture is that it happened to be Sharon Tate's first. It was being rewritten by Terry Southern and John Calley—not the original writers, of course—while Alexander Mackendrick, the director, and the cast, which included Tony Curtis and Claudia Cardinale, waited on a soundstage at MGM for the new script pages. Mike walked into Calley's office as he and Terry were working feverishly.

"Forgive me for interrupting, but may I ask you a technical question?"

"Sure," Calley replied.

"What happens if Mackendrick finishes the picture before you two finish the script?"

Don't Make Waves looked as if Mackendrick had.

Studios bring in as many writers on a script as they deem necessary. Recently, two friends, both excellent and highly regarded writers—Al Sargent and Darryl Ponicsan—found out over a social breakfast that they were both working simultaneously on the same screenplay. The director had not bothered to tell them.

George Oppenheimer was frequently hired by studios to polish screenplays. His screen credit always came after the other writers', so frequently, in fact, that he was introduced at Hollywood parties as "and George Oppenheimer."

Not only do writers, other than the original, work on scripts, but producers and directors, actors, and anyone else who happens to be around feel free to make changes. Writers, in fact, are treated with so little respect and rank so low in the Hollywood pecking order that they tell the story about an ambitious young extra on a picture who was so dumb that she slept with the writer. According to Julie Epstein, a veteran screenwriter and one of the best, writers invariably get seated in restaurants at tables next to the kitchen. The public think actors make up the words as they go along and directors often consider themselves "auteurs," a fighting word to every screenwriter.

Robert Riskin once sent 120 blank pages to Ernst Lubitsch, one of the industry's most respected and admired directors, with a covering note.

"Let's see you put some of your famous 'touches' on these."

There have been those exceedingly rare occasions when writers got more than their due.

DOUGLAS FAIRBANKS & MARY PICKFORD
in William Shakespeare's
THE TAMING OF THE SHREW

with additional dialogue by
Sam Taylor

When Mike Todd was killed in the crash of his private plane, it was front-page news in papers all over the world. Most, like the *Los Angeles Times,* I recall, went on for pages, detailing the producer's extraordinary career and life, including his marriage to Elizabeth Taylor. At the end of the extensive coverage, if at all, it was mentioned that a screenwriter, Arthur Cohen, had also died in the crash.

"I'm surprised," Billy Wilder wryly commented, "they didn't write, 'Additional dying by Arthur Cohen.'"

The dialogue in Brian De Palma's update of *Scarface,* starring Al Pacino in the role first played by Paul Muni, is so larded with obscenities that a Hollywood wit was moved to say, "The writing credit should've been 'Screenplay by Oliver Stone with additional fuck-yous by David Mamet.'"

The studios had their writers all working in the same building, where they

○ 197 ○

could be watched and controlled. William Faulkner asked if it would be all right if he did his writing at home. The studio agreed to make a rare exception—it was, after all, the great William Faulkner. Faulkner went home—to Mississippi.

The studio heads, I'm told, never had any understanding whatsoever of the creative process. They wanted to hear nothing but the constant, continuous pounding of typewriters, as if inspiration only came between nine and five. The immortal line in *Casablanca*—"Round up the usual suspects"—came, as an example, to Julie Epstein and his identical twin brother, Phil, as they were driving to the studio early one morning. Whenever Jack Warner saw the Epstein brothers on the lot he always said, "Hello, boys." Even after Phil died prematurely, Warner continued to greet Julie in the same way— "Hello, boys."

The Epsteins were brought to Hollywood by their friend Jerry Wald, the inspiration for Budd Schulberg's *What Makes Sammy Run?* When Wald went to work in

Hollywood as a young screenwriter, he said to the twins, "If I make it I'm going to send for you guys." Wald started at Warner Bros. at $50 a week rewriting scenes and soon worked his way up to $100. But now he was expected to actually write entire screenplays and he wasn't really that good a writer. So he sent a telegram to his friends the Epsteins: HOP A BUS.

When Leonard Spigelgass, who was already established in New York as a writer, came to Hollywood he changed his name for a short while to Leonard Sinclair. Leonard, who became a very good friend of mine, changed it back when his friends began calling him Upton Spigelgass.

At MGM the writers all worked in the Ince Building, where a disproportionate number of Hungarians, for reasons unknown to me, worked at their craft. There was a sign posted in the building that read BEING HUNGARIAN IS NOT ENOUGH. YOU MUST ALSO BE TALENTED.

Charles MacArthur, the playwright, who was definitely not Hungarian, was working on a screenplay at MGM. He used to get gas at the same filling station on his way to the studio and befriended the pump jockey—let's call him Joe Burke—who confided that he was in a lot of trouble financially and might lose his house. MacArthur went to the studio and told his producer that he was having trouble with the script and there was only one writer who could help him with it.

"Ben Hecht?"

"No, Joe Burke."

And so Burke came to the studio for ten weeks at $1000 a week and just sat in MacArthur's office all day doing absolutely nothing.

Writers, incidentally, never throw anything away. That famous line from *The General Died at Dawn*—"We could make such beautiful music together"—were words that Harold Clurman, the director, made Clifford Odets cut from his marvelous play *Awake and Sing*.

Otto Preminger, to his everlasting credit, was instrumental in breaking the insidious Hollywood blacklist. He hired

Dalton Trumbo, one of the Hollywood Ten who had spent nine months in jail for contempt of Congress, to write the screenplay of *Exodus*. But Otto wasn't completely satisfied with the first draft.

"A lot of the scenes are brilliant, but there are some that are quite dull."

"But, Otto," said Trumbo, "you have to have some dull scenes to make the brilliant ones stand out."

"Trumbo," Preminger responded, "you write all of them brilliant and I'll dull a few of them up with my direction."

George Axelrod's play *The Seven Year Itch* was a huge hit on Broadway and he became the hottest, most sought-after writer in Hollywood. He had a meeting with Sam Goldwyn, who wanted him to write the sequel of *The Secret Life of Walter Mitty*.

"I ran into your friend Billy Wilder last night," Goldwyn said as Axelrod entered his office.

"Oh, yes? Where?"

"At my house."

Goldwyn once said of a writer, "He's ridiculously overpaid but he's worth it."

Herman Mankiewicz, a legendary wit, was at a party where someone, as always, was sitting at the feet of the great Charlie Chaplin.

"Doesn't all that fawning and adulation bother him?" someone asked Mankiewicz.

"Not at all," Mankiewicz replied. "As a matter of fact, if no one's sitting at his feet he'll go someplace else in the room and stand where people are sitting."

In the old days when studios were still studios, there was always a table set aside in the commissary at lunch for the contract writers. And, of course, that was the table that was always the most fun.

Mankiewicz was lunching at the writers' table at Fox when he returned from New York after seeing Kaufman and Hart's *Merrily We Roll Along* on Broadway. Everyone was eager to hear from Mankiewicz, who had once been a theater critic, about the unconventionally structured play.

"In the first scene," Mankiewicz began, "we are introduced to the protagonist, who has had enormous success as a Broadway composer and who is now a wildly successful, wealthy Hollywood producer. He has a beautiful wife and an even more beautiful mistress. During the rest of the play, as it works its way backward in time to his youth, we discover how the son of a bitch got himself into such a terrible mess."

One day Loretta Young walked over to that same table carrying one of those coin collection cans for her pet Catholic charity.

"That'll cost you fifty cents," she said to Joe Mankiewicz, Herman's brother.

"What'll cost me fifty cents?"

"You took the name of the Lord in vain."

Mankiewicz dug into his pocket, fished out two quarters, and dropped them through the can's slot. Young thanked him and turned to go back to her nearby table.

"Oh, Loretta," Mankiewicz, a master of comic timing, called out to her.

"Yes?" she said, turning to face him.

"How much would it cost me if I told you to go fuck yourself?"

Julie Epstein once told me that the only actor who was ever welcome on a regular basis at the Warner Bros. writers' table was Errol Flynn, so fascinated were they all by Flynn's explicit accounts of his sexual escapades.

The ribbing writers gave each other was constant. The previously mentioned George Oppenheimer was asked by one of his fellow writers if he had ever been to Paris.

"Of course I have," replied Oppenheimer, a sophisticated world traveler.

"And do you speak French, George?"

"Certainly"

"Then would you mind passing the French bread?"

Television writers are the ones who work under the greatest pressure—especially the writers on comedy series.

Everett Greenbaum and Jim Fritzell replaced David Swift as the head writers of *Mr. Peepers* and the work they did week after week was just tremendous. Greenbaum had been a hotshot fighter pilot during the war and he had the teeth to go with it. They were really gorgeous. He smiled a lot and he drove fast sports cars. At the time, all the writers who worked for Fred Coe and Talent Associates— Paddy Chayefsky, Reggie Rose, Robert Alan Aurthur—worked in one big office. Greenbaum had one phobia: false teeth. He hated and feared them. "They smell," he used to say. Well, you can't drive a fast sports car and have great big beautiful teeth forever. He had a crash in his car and the worst happened: he knocked out one of his beautiful front teeth. For three weeks while he underwent dental work he never smiled. He wasn't Everett Greenbaum anymore. And then the day finally came. He walked into the office and flashed his million-dollar smile on everyone. "Hi, everybody!" And from the back of the office Fritzell said, "Everett, it smells terrible!"

Writers are not always fond of actors who improvise. When Harvey Miller would occasionally grow weary of our improvising scenes on *The Odd Couple* he'd send us a script with some blank pages. *"Mr. Randall and Mr. Klugman,"* Harvey would write, *"will dazzle us in this scene with their footwork."* We were doing a segment that had something to do with the Louis-Schmeling fight and we wanted a song about Schmeling's glass jaw. We yelled at Miller, who was on the phone, and asked him for a lyric. Without hesitation he sang back, "Vots on my face dot breaks a lot?/ My glass jaw."

One of the reasons the writing was so good on *The Odd Couple* was that we forced them to rewrite. Writers are like everyone else—they want to go home at night. As Dorothy Parker said, "I love to have written." But our writers stayed on at the studio until ten or eleven at night and Jack and I stayed with them.

The TV show was based, of course, on

Neil Simon's Broadway hit. Neil and his older brother Danny worked together, mostly on television, at the beginning of their careers and then went their separate ways. Danny and one of his subsequent writing partners, Martin Ragaway, were having a heated disagreement over a joke for a TV comedy special.

"Don't argue with me," Simon said, "I'm one of the best comedy writers in the business."

"Danny, you're not even the best in your family."

Good comedy writers are treasured. Sid Dorfman, one of the Burns and Allen show's top writers, decided he wanted to go off on his own and so he resigned. Burns was determined not to lose him. He called Dorfman into his office and turned on his vast charm, powers of persuasion, and humor. A master performer was at work.

"You're not just another writer, Sid, you're like a son to me and Gracie—the son we never had. If you left us it would be like losing a son. It would be . . ."

Dorfman was so embarrassed by now that he lowered his eyes and stared at the carpet.

"Sid," Burns continued, "I can't perform if you don't look at me."

There are some comedy writers who actually write very little but are brilliant on their feet. Harry Crane, one of the legendary comedy writers, was working for Jackie Gleason on the Great One's TV variety show. They always worked under enormous pressure and this particular week they were stuck for an idea.

"I've got it!" Crane said.

"Save me," said Gleason.

"There's only one question," Crane continued. "Have you, Jackie, got the guts to go out there onstage and do this joke?"

"What do you mean?"

"I'm telling you, Jackie, that this joke is so strong that nothing can follow it. You may actually have serious problems in the audience. There will be people, I promise you, who will have apoplexy from laughing, even heart attacks. That's how funny it is. So, the question is, does Jackie

Gleason have the confidence, the guts, to go out and do this joke?"

"I don't know, Harry," Gleason said. "Tell it to me."

And so Crane told the joke to Gleason.

"I don't think that's so funny," Gleason said.

"All right," said Crane, "I got another one."

Pat McCormick, the world's tallest comedy writer, and for years the head writer of the Johnny Carson show, was given a surprise birthday party by his friends. The party's theme was Polish. Just before they brought out the birthday cake and candles, everyone was handed a sheet of paper on which were printed the words of "Happy Birthday."

Jesse Owens, the great track star; Mantovani, the British conductor/arranger who was the first musician to sell more than one million stereo albums, and Dick Haymes died over the same weekend. Pat came into the office that Monday cursing the fates. "Just my luck! I just sold the network the biggest idea of my life—

the greatest special that's ever been on the air! It was going to star Dick Haymes, Mantovani, and Jesse Owens."

One of the only times Buck Henry, the straight-faced writer and frequent host of *Saturday Night Live,* has been known to have actually laughed out loud was when he and Mike were talking about Dick and Paul Sylbert, who are identical twins. Mike said that although he had known the motion-picture art directors for years, he could never tell them apart. I can't, either, for that matter.

"Oh," said Buck, "I can quite easily."

"You really know them that well?"

"Yes."

"Well," said Mike, "then you must know that one of them is adopted!"

○●○○●○

Growing

up in

Hollywood

and

elsewhere

○●○○●○

---○---

From the time he was a little boy, Warner LeRoy has had a weight problem. One day, so the story goes, as he watched a boyhood chum climb a tree on the LeRoy estate in Beverly Hills, Warner turned to his mother and said forlornly, "Gee, I wish I could do that."

"We'll get you a tutor," she replied.

---○---

GROWING UP IN Tulsa, Oklahoma, is a lot different, I can assure you, than it is in Hollywood. It strikes me that the kids it was the most difficult for were the child stars. Without exception they were exploited children who were deprived of their childhood. The English are much stricter than we are about children working on the stage and in films. Education isn't the problem, really, because they're all bright kids. They learn very, very quickly. The problem is, when do they play? When do they go outdoors? When do they just goof around and be children? Some of them defy all expectations and become very nice, seemingly normal, men and women, just ordinary, decent citizens. But many of them don't. When they reach their adulthood, they often revert to childhood and try to make up for the childhood they never had. They're often wild and irresponsible as adults. They've never played. I suppose it was ever so—think of Mozart. But almost all of these child stars have been written about at great length.

It's some of the sons and daughters of Hollywood's elite whom we'll deal with in this chapter. It strikes me as nothing less than remarkable that most of the ones I know seem so normal.

Warner LeRoy, the boniface of the late Maxwell's Plum and the Tavern on the Green in New York, was in many ways the prototypical Hollywood child. His mother, Doris, was the daughter of Harry, one of the three brothers Warner whose studio, as I've already noted, introduced "talkies." What many dismissed as a passing fad changed the business forever. Mervyn LeRoy, the director and producer, was Warner's father. It was Warner's Yorkshire terrier who was Dorothy's beloved Toto in his father's production of *The Wizard of Oz.*

Warner stammers, as did his father, who used to tell people to call him, "and, if no one answers, it's me." Warner was being unusually naughty on one occasion and his mother slapped him. Warner slapped her back and became so terrified that he ran up the stairs of their mansion into his room, slammed the door, and locked and barricaded it. Neither his mother, nor his father, nor his sister Linda, nor the manservants, nor the maid-servants could say or do anything to persuade him to come out. Hours went by.

How did they prevail on him? How was Warner finally enticed out of his room? Why, they sent for Warner's idol, the pied piper of Hollywood, Danny Kaye.

Warner's cousin Barbara, the daughter of Jack Warner, lived with her parents and sister on a huge estate in Beverly Hills, where most other mansions sit on surprisingly little land. As Barbara descended the grand stairway to greet a friend who had come to play, she said, "Shall we walk to the pool or take the car and chauffeur?"

Joe Mankiewicz was on the phone spatting with his wife, Rosa. She wanted the car and chauffeur to pick up their son, Chris, after school to take him on an errand.

"But I need the car and chauffeur," Mankiewicz said.

"It won't take very long," his wife persisted.

"God damn it," Mankiewicz said, putting an end to the discussion, "let him take taxis like other children!"

Budd Schulberg's cousin Barbara and her two sisters, the daughters of the powerful agent Sam Jaffe, went trick-or-treating every Halloween in the family limousine. Years later Barbara and her husband John Kohn, a movie writer and producer, whom I befriended in London when they were a part of that rather sizable enclave of expatriate Americans, were planning a birthday party for Sue, their five-year-old daughter, and some of her friends.

"Why don't we hire a clown or a musician?"

"Oh, Barbara," John demurred, "that's so Hollywood. I'll just bring home a picture from the studio and we'll run it."

John, incidentally, is the only person I know who has actually started a conversation by saying, "What I'm trying to say is . . ."

If you are left with the impression, as I am, that almost everyone in Hollywood's ruling hierarchy was related either by blood or marriage, it is a correct one. To this day the genealogies remain complicated and, at times, confusing, all the more so because of the extremely high divorce rate.

"My father can beat up your father," said one little Hollywood boy to another.

"Don't be ridiculous. Your father *is* my father."

A fear of abandonment is something all children, no matter where and whose, have in common. Jerry Hellman, the producer *(Midnight Cowboy, Coming Home, Mosquito Coast),* and his wife were driving in Beverly Hills with their four-year-old son, who was in the backseat of the car. As they turned a corner, the back door, which had not been properly closed, flew open and the little boy fell out. Hellman slammed on the brakes. Panic-stricken, he and his wife jumped out of the car and ran back toward their child. Unhurt, the boy ran toward them, his arms outstretched, tears streaming down his cheeks.

"Wait for me!" he cried out.

As someone who has not been blessed with children, I sometimes wonder at the unpredictability of children's reactions. One day the very witty and amusing English character actor Reginald Gardiner was on the set at Fox, a lot at which I have often worked, when he was called to the telephone. It was a call from his wife to tell him that their five-year-old son's pet turtle had suddenly died and that the boy was inconsolable. Gardiner went home during his lunch break and found the child still in tears.

"You know what we'll do?" he said. "We'll take a box of wooden matches, empty it, put some cotton in it, and put the little turtle inside. Then," he continued, "we'll paint the wooden matches white, dig a little hole right outside your bedroom window, put the box in the hole, cover it with dirt, and put the white matches around the hole like a picket fence."

By now Gardiner's son, very taken with the whole idea, had stopped crying. Father and son went to get the turtle and discovered that it was not dead after all. The boy looked up at his father, a momentary trace of surprise and disappointment in his expression. And then, with a gleam in his eye, he said, "Should we kill it?"

Sydney Chaplin, one of Charlie's two sons by the beautiful Lita Grey, was out on a bender one night in Palm Springs with Gary Crosby, one of Bing's many sons. As

Sydney was pouring his buddy into bed, Gary looked up at him forlornly and said, "Oh, Sydney, if you only knew what it was like to be the son of a famous man."

Nikki Lubitsch, whose father was the celebrated director Ernst of "the Lubitsch touch," was once told by her mother that she considered herself to be an exceptional parent because unlike most of Nikki's equally privileged contemporaries, she did not have a relief governess. When her regular Nanny had the day off, her mother actually took care of her.

While strolling on Rodeo Drive in Beverly Hills, Phil Silvers ran into his friend Sid Zelinka, the comedy writer, his wife, and his four-year-old daughter Blanche. When Silvers left, Zelinka said to his daughter "Do you know who that was?"

"No."

"He's an actor. He's on television."

"Is he a cat or a mouse?"

I know a famous Hollywood producer, once an agent, who was overheard giving Polonius-like advice to his son, who was just finishing his first movie as a producer:

". . . and if you don't like to lie, then you should have been a doctor."

After Dalton Trumbo, the screenwriter, spent nine months in jail for contempt of Congress, he moved with his family to Mexico, where he continued to write and sell screenplays to Hollywood studios under an assumed name. And what's more, they knew they were his scripts. In fact he won an Academy Award for one of those screenplays while he was still blacklisted. Nikola, his teenage daughter, fell in love with a Mexican boy who went to the same high school. Trumbo and his wife asked her when she was going to tell him that her father had been in jail. She would, she said, when the right time came.

"You know," Nikola said when the right time came, "my father was in jail for nine months. He was a political prisoner."

The boy, whose father was a Mexican politico, thought she was being boastful.

"Whose father wasn't?" he responded.

It amazes me how children are shaped by world events. Robert Alan Aurthur, the marvelous TV writer and producer whom I worked with on *Mr. Peepers,* had a son who was eleven years old in the sixties. He came home from school one afternoon bursting with excitement.

"Daddy, I've been elected vice-president of my class and if Enrique Silberbight is assassinated, I'm president!"

When Michael Douglas was eight, he wanted to go to the Beverly Hills Tennis Club with his father Kirk.

"But it'll be very boring for you watching a bunch of men play tennis."

Michael insisted.

"Okay, but I promise you it's not going to be any fun."

Father and son arrived at the club just as the pro was making good on a wager he had made with the screenwriter Charles Lederer that he could beat him at tennis while strapped to the leg of an elephant.

The state of American education being what it is, I find that kids today frequently have no knowledge at all of geography. Karen Medak, the seventeen-year-old daughter of director Peter Medak *(The Ruling Class),* was on a tour of Europe, the Middle East, and the Orient. It was a high-school graduation present from an enormously wealthy Saudi Arabian businessman and his wife. While driving with them in the south of France along the Mediterranean, she called Barbara Kohn in London on the car's telephone.

"Are you calling from the Corniche?" asked my friend Barbara, who was referring to the famous scenic road that laces its way along the cliffs above the sea.

"Oh, no," Karen replied, "I'm calling from the Mercedes."

Who but a privileged kid from Beverly Hills would even know that a Corniche is a Rolls-Royce model?

Hedda Hopper, the Hollywood gossip columnist, once told me that when she was still an actress she was making *Midnight* with Don Ameche, Claudette Colbert, and that greatest of all American actors, John Barrymore. Hedda's son Bill, then fifteen, asked his mother if he could come to the studio to meet Barrymore, his idol. She was hesitant because no one ever knew what Barrymore was going to say, especially after he had a drink or two. Young Bill persisted and Hedda eventually relented, but not before speaking to Barrymore.

"Now, Jack, you'll behave yourself, won't you? Bill's only fifteen and he's very impressionable."

Barrymore assured her and he was true to his word. He was utterly charming to the lad. (Barrymore also knew Bill's father, the noted actor De Wolf Hopper, who was married four times, to women named Nedda, Hedda, Edna, and Etta.) Barrymore went out of his way to treat Hedda's son as an honored guest, and she was delighted. Toward the end of the day Barrymore said, "Bill, what do you want to do, my boy?"

"I want to be an actor," he replied.

"I don't like to hear that, son, I really don't. And I'll tell you why," Barrymore began. "When I was a young man I was hired by Willie Collier, whom many thought the finest actor of his day, to join his company for a tour of Australia in *The Boys of Company B.* It was a wonderful experience. Wonderful! He taught me so much. Our last stop was Sydney, where we were booked for six weeks. I made friends there with a young Australian who was the lover of a whorehouse madam."

Hedda coughed and sputtered. Try as she did, there was no stopping Barrymore.

"He asked me to move into the bordello with him and of course I did. And those, my boy, were the six most glorious weeks of my life—an orgy every night. On our last night, the whores threw a lavish party for me—champagne, oysters—a banquet. They threw themselves all over me and begged me not to go back to the States. We partied all night long and my friend said, 'Jack, why go back to the rat race tomorrow? Stay here. I can find you your own madam and you can move into her whorehouse with her.' And, my boy, as I look back on my life, I realize that that's what I should have done. And that's what you should do.''

Much to Hedda's relief Bill Hopper did not take his idol's advice. He became an actor and, to the best of my knowledge, never toured Australia. He's best remembered for his running role as the investigator opposite Raymond Burr on the Perry Mason TV series.

I took my twelve-year-old nephew Ben onto the set of *Marathon Man* out at Warner Bros. At the time, Jack Klugman and I were playing in *The Odd Couple* at the Shubert Theatre in Century City and I wanted Olivier to see it. Olivier saw me, came over, and after I introduced him to Ben, he put his hands on my shoulders and said, ''I fucking well intend to see your fucking show and I fucking well will.''

When we left, Ben was staggered. ''Did you hear that word Olivier used?''

"Oh," I said, "he just used that as an intensifier."

Every night after that when I'd come home from the theater, Ben would ask me if Olivier had come to see the show. After a week or two I said, "Ben, he's not coming."

"Would Laurence Olivier lie? Would Laurence Olivier use *fucking* as an intensifier if he didn't intend to come?"

I am no less intrigued by the behavior of children outside the Hollywood community, the offspring of, for the most part, less celebrated people, mostly in New York, who are in some way or another connected with show business.

At age eight Tony, the son of agent Robby Lantz and his wife Sherlee, was teasingly asked by his parents whom he would choose to live with if they should ever get divorced.

Without hesitating for a moment, he replied, "Dick and Evie Avedon."

Alan Kyle was ten when he said to his mother, lyricist-librettist Betty Comden, "I want to be a nonconformist like every-body else.''

Mike was shooting a documentary with the extraordinary French skier Jean-Claude Killy in Zermatt, Switzerland, and sent his three nephews a postcard with a picture on it of that most mountainous-looking of all mountains, the Matterhorn. What limited knowledge of geography the boys, who lived in Palo Alto, had was gleaned from television and an occasional visit to Disneyland, but certainly not from school. When the postcard arrived, one of his nephews said to his mother ''Oh, do they have a Matterhorn in Switzerland too?''

The founder of the Czechoslovakian film industry, Josef Auerbach, fled to this country with his wife and children when Hitler's legions invaded his homeland. A man of enormous wit, Auerbach once con-fided to a friend, ''The only pleasure I ever got from my three children was their gov-ernesses.'' His son, Norbert, grew up to be the head of United Artists and is immor-talized in Steven Bach's wonderful book

Final Cut, which chronicles the disaster of Michael Cimino's *Heaven's Gate.*

Many a story has come out of verbal misunderstandings: "Laddy's dead," said Martha, the wife of Jay Emmett, a former Warner Bros. executive, over the phone. How, she asked her husband, was she going to tell their seven-year-old son that his beloved dog had been run over?

"Just be straight with him," Emmett counseled. "He can take it."

His mother told the boy when he came home from school. He listened without saying a word and then went out to play. How strange, his mother thought, that he showed absolutely no emotion. When the boy came home later, his concerned mother said, "Darling, did you understand what I told you? Laddy's dead. He was run over by an automobile." The boy burst into tears.

"Laddy? I thought you said Daddy!"

Childhood is full of such confusions and misunderstandings. When George Axelrod was a boy growing up in New York, he thought he heard on the radio that

Johnny White's mother was going to play Tarzan on the screen. Who, he wondered, was Johnny White and how come his mother was going to play Tarzan? He had, of course, misheard Johnny Weissmuller.

I had a wonderful teacher in high school—Miss Ronan—Isabel Ronan. She used to read Stanislavsky to us. Back in those days it seemed to me that almost everyone who was great, the people whom you respected most, were gentiles with three names—William Lyon Phelps, Joseph Wood Krutch, Nicholas Murray Butler, Herbert Bayard Swope, Robert Maynard Hutchins. There was another theatrical group in high school that excluded me. Their teacher was Mr. Cleveland and they put on such things as *Aria da Capo* by Edna St. Vincent Millay, another one of those names. I used to hear Mr. Cleveland's students talk about things I knew nothing about. And, it seemed, they were always quoting a particular man with three wonderful names: Theodore Ards Mundley. I thought that when I got to be as sophisticated as they, I, too, would know who this man was. Not until I was in college did I discover *Theatre Arts* monthly.

Of all the confusions and mysteries of childhood, sex is certainly the biggest. Jamie, the eldest child of Leonard Bernstein, was eleven when her mother Felicia came home from New York's Doctors Hospital with her newborn sister, Nina. Several days later Jamie entered her mother's bedroom and asked, once again, how babies are made. Felicia patiently explained and answered all of Jamie's questions.

"And, Mummy, every time you do 'it' do you have a baby?"

Felicia went even more deeply into the intricacies and mysteries of conception. As Jamie was leaving the room, she turned and, almost as an afterthought, asked her mother one more question.

"Mummy, did you and Daddy do 'it' *before* or *after* you went into the hospital?"

Mike Elliott, who has directed me in more than one television commercial, is a man of enthusiasm, curiosity, and other admirable traits which he has passed on to his four children. When his son Bobby was five, a friend of the family took him to a store on Fire Island and bought him a lot of candy. While walking home, Bobby stuffed himself with the sweets and became ill. It was, in fact, his first experience with throwing up. When he finished what is for most children, and adults as well, a decidedly traumatic experience, Bobby was bursting with curiosity. He looked up and asked in his Munchkin-like little voice, "What was that?"

Finally, a crossover story: one that pertains in part to Hollywood but which is about people who lived in a small town in New Jersey. John Calley, until recently the head of production at Warner Bros., has a younger brother who was acquired in a most unusual way. Calley's parents were divorced and his father, a used-car dealer, remarried. The new Mrs. Calley, unable to conceive, wanted a child.

"Okay," Mr. Calley said, "I'll see what I can do."

He went to his used-car lot and let the

fellows know that he was looking for an infant. Some days later a man walked onto the lot carrying a very malnourished-looking baby.

"What do you want for the kid?" Calley's father asked.

"I want a thirty-nine Chevy convertible."

"For that? Are you crazy? He's got scabs all over him. I'll tell you what—I'll give you a thirty-eight Ford hardtop. Take it or leave it."

"Will you throw in a heater?"

"Okay, it's a deal," and they shook hands.

And that's how the senior Calley acquired a baby for his wife. But according to John, whenever his little brother misbehaved in any way, his father would always say to his wife, "I told you that kid was no thirty-nine Chevy convertible."

The
celebrity
connection

A minor screen actor was put in Malibu jail one Saturday night to sleep off a drunk. When he awoke the next day, his cellmate was staring at him.

"Are you in the movies?"

"Yes," the hung-over actor responded.

"Well, I screwed Peggy Ann Garner's maid."

THERE ARE PEOPLE who have an overwhelming, seemingly irresistible need—indeed a compulsion—to make a connection, direct or indirect, with a celebrity. Exactly why this is so is best left to others to explain, but I know— often from personal experience, sometimes bitter—that the condition is by no means uncommon.

The first connection I ever made with a celebrity was in my hometown, Tulsa, Oklahoma, and it was with Katharine Cornell. I was fourteen and went backstage, after seeing her superb production of *Romeo and Juliet,* to get her autograph, for which she charged twenty-five cents. That's what she charged everyone. She gave the money to the Red Cross. Cornell had this mean woman standing beside her—Gertrude Macey—who took the quarters. That same woman was mean to me some years later when I worked with Cornell. Cornell borrowed someone's pen to sign her autograph—it may have been mine—and, brash adolescent that I was, I said, "Someday I'll give you mine." And she responded, "Autograph or pen?"

Celebrityhood definitely has its advantages, but sometimes it isn't easy. As a rule people are very nice about it when they approach you, as long as you do what they want.

"Mr. Randall," an old lady said to me on a bus in New York, "can I have your autograph?"

Now, someplace like a bus is a bad place to start giving autographs.

"I hope you understand," I said, trying my best to be gracious, "but if I do it for you, everyone else will ask me."

"Oh, don't be conceited," she said, "nobody else recognizes you."

A little man came up to me in my gym and said in some strange accent, "Tony Randalls?"

"Yes."

"You're Tony Randalls?"

"Yes."

He then turned to the man who runs the gym and said, "Who is that guy?"

"He's Tony Randall."

"He told me he was Tony Randall*s*. I didn't believe him."

People, by the way, often say "Hello, Felix" when they see me. It's all those *Odd Couple* reruns. The more formal ones say "Hello, Mr. Unger." When I was doing *Love, Sidney* they'd often say "Hello, Sidney." Jack Klugman tells me that he's invariably greeted as "Quincy."

Bob Hope told me he was on a plane when a man crept up behind him and whispered, "Are you he?"

There are people who feel they have

the right to say anything they want to celebrities.

Fred Clark was one of those marvelous character actors who worked all the time. His face was familiar to millions, but the public always had difficulty connecting it with his name. He had been one of the regulars on the Burns and Allen television show for years when he decided to leave it. A couple of years later a fan not only recognized him but knew his name.

"Aren't you Fred Clark?"

"Yes," Clark beamed.

"You used to be on the Burns and Allen show, right?"

"Right," Clark said, still beaming.

"Well, Mr. Clark, I gotta tell you, it's a much better show now without you."

Fritz Weaver is another one of those instantly recognizable character actors who work all the time but whom the public often has difficulty naming.

"Aren't you Fritz Weaver?" a New York City taxi driver said to him as he got into his cab.

"Why, yes, I am," Weaver responded

with a measure of satisfaction. "How would you know?"

"I'm a trivia buff."

Occasionally, you even get that kind of treatment from people you know. A dear friend, the widow of George Marek, once the head of RCA Victor records, told me that she had just seen *Murder on the Orient Express,* in which Albert Finney played Hercule Poirot. I had played the Belgian detective in another picture, *The Alphabet Murders.*

"How was he in my part?" I asked.

"Worse than you."

I told that to Finney and he didn't laugh.

It depends on the situation, but sometimes a celebrity can handle an aggressive fan in a superb way.

Cary Grant and Peter Stone were having dinner when a fan came to their table and asked Grant for his autograph. Grant asked him very politely to please come back when he had finished his meal.

The fan became indignant. "Who do you think you are?"

"We both know who I am, dear boy," Grant responded. "Who the hell are you?"

Barbra Streisand was having lunch with some friends on a rainy summer Sunday in a little restaurant called the Quiet Clam in East Hampton, Long Island. People at the other tables were all abuzz: was it or wasn't it Streisand? One man could stand the uncertainty no longer. He got up from his table, approached hers, leaned over, and said, somewhat tentatively, "You're not Barbra Streisand. . . ."

Streisand put her hand up to her bosom and said, "I'm not?"

I have observed over the years, incidentally, that the fans who interrupt you in the middle of your meal—"I hate to bother you but . . ."—never do it until they've finished their own.

I ran into a young actress, Judy Graubart, at theater one evening. She wanted my advice about a voice teacher and came over to me at intermission. We talked vocal technique for about five minutes and then Judy went back to her seat. As I sat down, the woman seated next to me, a stranger, said in a rather challenging tone, "Well, what was that all about?"

José Ferrer lives in an apartment house just down West Fifty-seventh Street from the Russian Tea Room. While riding down the crowded elevator in his building, a fellow passenger, a rather matronly but reasonably attractive woman wearing glasses, started speaking to him.

"Aren't you José Ferrer?"

"Yes I am."

"Oh, Mr. Ferrer, I'm such a big admirer of yours. I have been for so many years. Is it true that you're uncircumcised?"

"Madam . . ." Ferrer sputtered.

"Oh, please let me see," the woman went on.

Ferrer bolted out of the door when the elevator reached the ground floor, ran across the lobby, and out onto the street. The woman was in hot pursuit.

"Oh, Mr. Ferrer," the woman continued, "please take it out. Please. Take it out. Take it out."

"Madam," Ferrer, extremely flustered, said, "I really don't—"

And at that moment the ardent fan revealed "herself." It was Dustin Hoffman in his *Tootsie* makeup and wardrobe, on his way to the Russian Tea Room to film that unforgettable scene in which he tells his agent that he's going to read for a woman's part on a soap opera.

On occasion people simply will not take no for an answer to a request for an autograph. Robert Mitchum, one of the freest of all Hollywood spirits, was strolling down the Champs-Elysée when a French fan started badgering him.

"Mr. Lancastaire, Mr. Lancastaire . . . may I pleez have your autograph?"

Mitchum kept walking but the Frenchman persisted until Mitchum finally relented. He took the pen and piece of paper the Frenchman offered him and wrote *"Kiss my ass"* and signed it Burt Lancaster.

Mistaken identity happens quite a lot. Marty Ransohoff and Mike were having a business meeting over drinks with Richard Burton after a matinee of *Hamlet.* It was at the height of Burton's celebrity and there were several hundred women standing on the sidewalk outside the bar of the Piccadilly Hotel peering in through the window. After Richard left to join Elizabeth for dinner at Sardi's, Ransohoff and Mike lingered at the bar for a while. A woman came up to Mike and said, "Mr. Burton, can I have your autograph?"

"I'm not Richard Burton."

"Oh, please, Mr. Burton. I'd appreciate it so much."

"But I'm telling you, I'm not Richard Burton. Really."

"Oh, come on, Richard, give her your autograph," Ransohoff said.

And so Mike, who looks nothing whatsoever like Burton, took her *Playbill* and signed it.

I simply don't understand why someone would want the autograph of a celebrity when she doesn't even know what he looks like.

Quite a few people have come up to Mike thinking he was Burt Bacharach. At one of those big charity dinners in Los Angeles, Zsa Zsa Gabor, whom Mike had never met, came over to him and said, "Give me a big kiss, darling." So he gave her a big kiss and threw in a squeeze, the devil!

"Who do you think I am?" he asked Zsa Zsa after he had his way with her.

"Why you're Burt Bacharach, darl— oh, no . . ." she said, starting to giggle, "you're not."

She was very good humored about it.

Introduced to Bacharach sometime after that, Mike told him the story and how often this has happened. Bacharach looked at him blankly. Mike then said to him, "Do you mean to tell me a lot of people don't come up to you and ask if you aren't Mike Mindlin?" He looked at Mike even more blankly.

Two women came up to Arnold Stang, the short and very plain-looking actor, when he was lunching with a friend in the Polo Lounge of the Beverly Hills Hotel.

"You're, you're . . ." one of the women said, pointing at him.

"Robert Stack."

"You see," the woman said to her companion, "I told you he was."

At theater one night, just moments before the first-act curtain, a man all the way across the orchestra stood up, pointed at me, and shouted "You—what's your name?"

I was walking down the street and as I passed a woman who was walking her dog, she turned to the animal and said, "Look! Look! Tony Randall."

Stars like Katharine Hepburn and Paul Newman have a hard-and-fast rule: no autographs at all.

When Hepburn was in Venice filming *Summertime,* Mike saw her spend at least ten minutes politely turning down four nuns.

"Wouldn't it have been a lot easier if you had given them your autograph?" Mike asked.

"No," she said. It was the principle of the thing, as it also is for Paul Newman.

Someone came up to me recently as I was walking down Fifty-seventh Street and said, "Isn't it awful? People recognize you wherever you go and they won't give you any privacy." This he says while he's invading my privacy. It's something you have to live with. It comes with the territory. There used to be the Metropolitan Diagnostic Institute in New York which was supported by all the theatrical unions: SAG, AFTRA, Equity. Any member could go once a year for a free checkup. They had a whole floor in the Paramount Building. You went from room to room and there was a specialist in each of them who'd examine you—heart, lungs, ears, eyes—everything. There must've been thirty doctors. This particular year when I got to the proctologist, he was a young Cuban who spoke with a very heavy accent. I got up on the table and assumed that very humiliating position on my hands and knees. As the doctor examined me, he said, "You look very familiar to me."

As we know only too well from the

murder of John Lennon, there is the distinct possibility of danger when a stranger approaches.

My late friend David Niven was working on a picture in the south of Spain, when someone he had barely known back in the old days approached him on the marble steps of his hotel one evening after dinner. The man, it seems, had been harboring some long-standing imagined grievance. He started upbraiding Niven, who just stood there listening, nonchalant and debonair as always, with his hands in his pockets. Finally Niven said to him, "You're a cunt," an expression that British men use only when they're insulting other men or themselves. Very sexist, to be sure, as if it were the worst thing anyone could possibly be. The man continued his abusive tirade and once again Niven, without raising his voice, said, "You're a cunt."

Undaunted, the man continued and Niven once more said, "You're a cunt."

With that the man suddenly slugged Niven and sent him sprawling on the marble steps, his hands still in his pockets.

Niven, who was big, strong, and very brave—an oft-decorated war hero, in fact —did not return the blow.

"But, David—why not?"

"Well, after all," he said, the voice of reason and of that highly developed sense of British fair play, "I did call him a cunt three times."

The late character actor Charles Butterworth (some say it was Roland Young) was riding on a train opposite a man who was staring at him with that unmistakable I-know-I've-seen-you-somewhere look. An extremely shy person, as so many actors are, Butterworth buried his face deep into the newspaper he was reading. His fellow passenger could tolerate the frustration no longer. He stuck his hand out and said, "How do you do. I'm Joe Smith from Abilene, Kansas."

"So am I," Butterworth replied.

I was walking down Madison Avenue, saw a beautiful tie in a window, and walked into the haberdashery. The guy was agog.

"Oh, Tony Randall in my shop! I

never thought! Oh, would you do me one big favor? Would you talk to my wife? She's such a big fan of yours!"

He calls his wife on the phone and makes me talk to her. He flattered me so that I bought three ties and a couple of shirts. I didn't have enough money, and I asked him if he'd take a check.

"Can I see some identification?"

Even stranger is something that happened in the Ginger Man in Beverly Hills, where Patrick O'Neal, who owns the restaurant with Carroll O'Connor, was dining with Robert Halmi, a producer, and Mike. When they finished dinner, Patrick went upstairs to do some work while Halmi and Mike remained at the table talking over coffee. A woman, unknown to either of them, came over to the table and interrupted them without so much as an excuse-me.

"Where's Patrick?" she asked.

"Upstairs in his office," Halmi replied.

"How long is he going to be there?" she asked rather impatiently.

"About a half hour," Halmi said.

"He promised me his autograph, you know, and I've sent for a taxi," she went on, looking at her wristwatch. "It'll be here any minute."

"Well, what do you want us to do about it?" Mike asked.

She thought for a moment.

"Why don't *you* sign it?" she said, handing Mike a pen and a menu.

Mike wasn't sure he understood her.

"You mean," he said in utter amazement, "you want me to sign *his* name?"

"Yes," she replied, as if she were making absolute sense, "just sign 'Patrick O'Neal' and right under it put 'per whatever your name is.' "

That woman, I assume, must have one helluva autograph collection—Julius Caesar, Jesus Christ, Alexander the Great . . .

Yes, people do strange things. I was in London at a matinee and saw Dustin Hoffman sitting alone a few rows behind me. It was soon after he had won the Oscar for *Kramer vs. Kramer.* I got up and sat down in the empty seat next to him. In the intermission—the interval as the English say—a band of teenage American tourists spotted Dustin and swarmed all over him to get his autograph. They ignored me. The next day at another matinee, I saw the same group and they swarmed all over me.

"Why didn't you ask me yesterday when I was with Dustin Hoffman?"

"Oh," one of the girls replied, "we didn't think you knew him."

John Barrymore was purchasing a bauble in Cartier's in New York when he was at the height of his fame.

"Charge it, please."

"Your name?" the saleswoman asked politely.

"Barrymore," he replied politely.

"And how do you spell it?"

Barrymore spelled it for her.

"And your first name, please?"

"Ethel!"

During the period when *Inherit the Wind* was closed and we were rehearsing with Paul Muni's replacement, Melvyn

Douglas, I was walking to the theater when a stranger stopped me.

"How's Paul's eye?"

"I understand he's going to be all right."

"How's Mel going to be in the part?"

"Fine."

"What's Wally going to be doing now that *Peepers* is going off the air?"

"I don't know."

"Okay, Tony," the man said as he departed, "I'll see you around."

A perfect stranger and the guy used four first names. As soon as he said, "How's Paul's eye?" I knew he didn't know him. Anyone who knew him called him Muni. Muni Weisenfreund—that was his real name. He changed it when he left the Yiddish theater.

Just to put it all in perspective I'll conclude with a story about Ingrid Bergman. "And what are you going to do with my autograph?" she asked an eight-year-old boy.

"I'll take it home and copy it in a book."

Gathering places

---○---

A Hollywood couple's beloved dog died and they actually gave it a funeral at which George Jessel, the master of the eulogy, spoke. Jessel had everyone in tears, including Jack Benny. The next day at the Hillcrest Country Club, Benny told everyone at the comedians' table, "I've known that animal for years and until Jessel's eulogy I had no idea how much the dog had done for Israel."

---○---

THE SINGLE BEST source of stories I know of on the West Coast is the famous comedians' table at the Hillcrest Country Club, where until fairly recently such comedians as Jack Benny, George Burns, George Jessel, Milton Berle, and an assortment of their cronies lunched together every day. Groucho once said that the average age at the table was deceased.

The Hillcrest is one of those places where people in show business flock together. There are, of course, others: the Polo Lounge at the Beverly Hills Hotel, Musso & Frank's on Hollywood Boulevard, and Nate-n-Al's delicatessen, where the conversation is as big an attraction as the food, are a few of the places that have remained ever popular at breakfast and lunch. And then there are the egalitarian studio commissaries where the food has always been dreadful but moderately priced and in which dress extras, secretaries, and file clerks rub elbows at lunch with studio heads and stars.

Fashions in restaurants change, especially at dinner, perhaps more rapidly in trendy Hollywood than elsewhere. But some, like Chasen's, especially on Sunday evenings, endure.

In New York, Sardi's, I suppose, in the heart of the theater district, and Elaine's are still "in." Orso's, right next door to Joe Allen's, on Forty-sixth Street west of perilous Eighth Avenue on Restaurant Row, is the current favorite hangout for dinner and after-theater. At lunch the Russian Tea Room predominates. The Hotel Edison's coffee shop, affectionately known as the Polish Tea Room, is a lot cheaper and has great sandwiches. Breakfasts are simply not a factor because New Yorkers in my world seldom if ever make breakfast dates with anyone but early-rising Californians.

As for the once-great delis—the Stage and the Carnegie, which once reigned supreme—very little of their former glory survives but the stories.

Hillcrest, like so many other Jewish country clubs in communities across the nation, was founded because the best local country club refused to accept Jews. Hillcrest's founding members were determined to outdo the L.A. Country Club in every way and they did—oil was discovered in the middle of the golf course and the wells are still pumping.

Danny Thomas was a regular at the comedians' table for more than twenty-five years, but Danny, a Catholic, wasn't a member. One day at lunch Thomas gave his fellow comedians a lecture.

"You're just as bigoted as they are at the L.A. club. They won't take in Jews, you won't accept gentiles. You both ought to be ashamed."

They took Thomas's words to heart and changed the club's bylaws. But they wouldn't admit Danny.

"If we're going to take in gentiles, at least they should look like gentiles."

Among the enduring legends of Hollywood is the size of Milton Berle's penis. Some fellow members of Hillcrest came to him at the comedians' table and said there was a new member who insisted that his was bigger and, what's more, he was willing to bet on it. Would Berle, they asked, accept the challenge and meet the upstart in the locker room?

"All right," said Berle wearily, "but I'm telling you now, I'm going to wear a towel and I'm only going to show enough of it to win."

Jack Benny was George Burns's pigeon. Burns could say almost anything and Benny would get hysterical. "Jack, we're going to be at Jeanette MacDonald's together later and you have to promise me you won't start laughing if she offers to sing after dinner." Throughout lunch Burns kept saying it. "Now, Jack, please behave yourself tonight. For God's sake, don't laugh if Jeanette offers to sing." And so, of course, immediately after dinner Jeanette said, "Shall we take our coffee in the music room . . . ?"

It may come as a surprise, but of all the comedians who were regulars at that fabled table, George Jessel was regarded as the funniest.

Not too long after the end of World War II, the main topic of conversation at lunch one day was Russia and whether or not it had the atomic bomb. All but one were in agreement that it was highly unlikely that such a backward, agrarian society was capable of so formidable a technological achievement. George Jessel was the lone dissenter at the table.

"Listen," he opined from his show-business perspective, "just because they dance sitting down . . ."

A member of Hillcrest supposedly developed a salve that when applied to the erect penis prevented premature ejaculation. He brought a tube to Groucho at the comedians' table, so the story goes, and a few days later inquired if it worked.

"I don't know," Groucho replied, "I came putting it on."

Some years later Hillcrest honored Groucho at one of those dinners at which people make tributes. As he listened to a lengthy recital of his achievements, Groucho turned to his neighbor on the dais and sighed. "I'd trade all that for one good erection."

Thanks to my friendship with Groucho I got to eat at Hillcrest's comedians' table a number of times. Groucho and I originally met one evening at Chasen's not too long after I went to Hollywood to make my first picture. Groucho was dining with Steve Allen, who introduced us. We exchanged a pleasant word or two and then I went to my table. Groucho sent his empty dinner plate over to me with a single strand of spaghetti on it.

"With Mr. Marx's compliments," the

waiter said as he placed the plate before me.

Groucho subsequently invited me to dinner at his house.

"Hello, Randall, how are you?" he greeted me at the door, shaking my hand and tickling my palm with his middle finger, the way we all did as little schoolboys. I wasn't feeling very well and apologized.

"I may get sick and ruin your party."

"You did that just by showing up."

Groucho and I got to know each other pretty well. When they syndicated *You Bet Your Life,* the kids of this country discovered him. It was a most remarkable comeback. My nephew Ben was besotted with Groucho. He had Groucho posters all over his room. I was having dinner with Groucho at Chasen's and I brought along my little tape recorder.

"Groucho, my sister's boy, Ben, is twelve years old. If you'd just say hello to him it would really be a good deed."

"Hello, Ben," he said in that absolutely original way of his, "you son of a bitch."

I mailed the cassette to Ben and he took it to school and all his pals heard the one and only Groucho call him a son of a bitch. You can just imagine what that did for Ben's social standing. When Groucho was dying, I took Ben to meet him. Groucho was at home in his room in a hospital bed. A TV set was hanging from the ceiling and he was watching a Mike Douglas show I'd taped two weeks before.

"Oh," Groucho said as we entered, "I was watching you on the tube. You were singing like a thrush."

He insisted on getting out of bed to shake Ben's hand and his pajama bottoms fell down.

"I go for laughs," he said.

Groucho was always in character. He was always Groucho. He said funny things all the time and it was almost always a form of insult. Someone he was dining with at Chasen's said to him, "You changed the art of verbal comedy and

9

It's not polite to point, I know, but here I am as Agatha Christie's Hercule Poirot, doing just that with Robert Morley in *The Alphabet Murders*. My nose, please note, is a trifle pointy, too.

Ah, the sacrifices one must make for art: movies with three of Hollywood's reigning sex queens—Marilyn Monroe (*Let's Make Love*), Kim Novak (*Boys' Night Out*), and Jayne Mansfield (*Will Success Spoil Rock Hunter?*). That jacket I'm wearing in the scene with Jayne belonged to Mickey Hargitay, the Hungarian body builder. So did Jayne.

10

11

12

13

Actors in movies are not permitted to do their own stunts, simply because if they are hurt doing something a double could do, the insurance company will not pay. But on the last day of shooting, the studio doesn't care anymore. In *The Mating Game*, the director, George Marshall, wanted Debbie Reynolds and me to jump out of a second-story window into this haystack. I was scared but Debbie, barely a month after having a child, was game and so I had to. We did it four times before Marshall was satisfied. Then I noticed a stunt man sitting off to the side in my costume. "What is he here for?" I asked. Marshall said, "In case you got hurt." The pig in Debbie's arms, incidentally, used a double.

14

15

SMOKING: Before I stopped and after.

14. *The Billy Rose Theatre Collection, The New York Public Library at Lincoln Center*

15. *© 1970, Paramount Pictures Corporation. All Rights Reserved*

Johnny Carson and I at our closest. Actually,
Johnny, try as he might, couldn't hear the
ringing in my ear. I hear it all the time. It's a
condition called tinnitus and there's nothing
that can be done for it.

Courtesy NBC Photography

17

New heights in chutzpah: me singing with
Sherrill Milnes, the great baritone of the
Metropolitan Opera.

Harpo changed the art of mime. What did Chico ever contribute?"

"Chico," Groucho replied, "introduced gonorrhea to the Orpheum vaudeville circuit."

Betty Comden introduced Frederic Morton to Groucho at Chasen's as the "man who wrote *The Rothschilds.*"

"Did they ever write back?"

Groucho once told Betty at Romanoff's, a Hollywood restaurant no longer in existence, that his pal, Goody Ace, was growing old. "He no longer buys jumbo-size toothpaste. In fact he won't buy a long-playing record."

For a time Ma Maison, another restaurant no longer in existence, was the Hollywood "in" crowd's favorite. It was so "in" that it actually had an unlisted phone number! Neil Simon grabbed the check there and his five guests continued their animated conversation until they noticed that Neil was taking an unduly long time signing. Finally he looked up with a dumb expression on his face and asked "What's fifteen percent of $4,879.29?"

It was that same evening at Ma Maison when Mike saw Richard Burton for the last time. Richard was on the wagon and looking very well. He beckoned Mike over to his table.

"Do I owe you any money, luv?"

"Yes, Richard, you owe me a fortune."

Richard laughed. If Mike had instead chosen to say that Burton owed him some reasonable amount, he's certain he would've been paid then and there, such were the gaps in what had once been a prodigious memory. Although Mike doesn't agree, I think Richard must've had some sense of impending doom and was settling accounts. Six months later he died in Switzerland.

While the food in studio commissaries is never notable, the company and conversation very often are. The first advice I was given in Hollywood was from David Niven: never eat in a studio commissary. David, who would often remind me that he was not English but Scottish, brought his lunch to the studio every day in a brown paper bag and ate in his dressing room.

If you're working at a studio for any length of time, as I often have, you stop eating in the commissary because the menu is pretty much the same every day. More often than not, over the years, I would follow David's advice and fix my own lunch in the dressing room: a can of tuna, and a glass of white wine. The only reason ever to go to the commissary was for the fun. The company was always convivial and stimulating.

When I was under contract to Fox they cast me in *The Young Lions* with Brando and Clift, the two best American actors I have seen. I was excited beyond containment. Everything was set until I was called into the producer's office and told I was being replaced by Dean Martin, who had just split with Jerry Lewis. It was an MCA power play. The super-agency represented Brando and Clift as well as Martin, and so their client was in the picture and I was out. Anyway, after that happened, MCA's man at the studio—I've forgotten his name—used to greet me effusively whenever we ran into each other in the commissary. "Hiya, Tony! How are you?" this very pleasant guy who had knifed me would always say. As I'd see him coming near my table, I'd look up to greet him. It became a habit. If he'd pass by without saying hello, my feelings would actually be hurt! Oh, Hollywood!

Delicatessens on both coasts have always been wellsprings of funny stories. They sell the food that one wit, unknown to me, said has killed more Jews than Hitler. Jewish culture is 5,748 years old and Chinese culture is 4,487 years old, and thus, according to Howard Albrecht, a comedy writer I know, we have one of the most intriguing of all anthropological mysteries: How did Jews survive for more than a thousand years without Chinese food?

Where but in Hollywood would a Chinese restaurant, Chin Chin, remain closed on Yom Kippur, while Greenblatt's, a delicatessen on the Strip, remained open?

Marvin Davis, who once owned

Twentieth Century-Fox, spends a lot of time in Nate-n-Al's, the Hollywood community's favorite delicatessen. Davis, an exceedingly large man and a voracious eater, ordered some smoked whitefish. Kay, the waitress with the fastest mouth west of New York's Carnegie Deli, brought him an entire fish that extended from one end of the table to the other. Davis, not up to his usual trencherman standards on that particular day, picked at the fish and asked Kay to remove it.

"There's a tow-away charge, you know."

Larry Gelbart says there's a disease that strikes Jews as they grow old. They're overcome with an irresistible, insatiable desire for pastrami, corned beef, and dill pickles. It's called Nate-n-Alzheimer's disease.

And now to New York and its restaurants and delis.

During World War II when meat was rationed, Mike asked a waiter at the Carnegie Delicatessen if he could order a roast beef sandwich.

"You could order it," the waiter replied in his Yiddish accent, "but you vouldn't get it."

I love those answers. They're so typically New York.

I was giving someone at Zabar's a takeout order over the phone. I gave him my street address and apartment number —"6D, for David."

"How do you like dat? I put down D for dog."

Every now and then those types get their comeuppance. When Walter Matthau was a struggling young actor in the theater, he went to Zabar's with his buddy Gene Saks, now a very successful director but then still an actor. Matthau, badly in need of a shave, was dressed accordingly. He pointed to some smoked fish in the display case and said to the counterman, who was busy sharpening his knife, "That fish there. . . ."

"The sturgeon?"

"Yeah."

○ 270 ○

"It's eight dollars a quarter of a pound," the counterman said very patronizingly, barely deigning to look at Matthau.

"I'll take a hundred pounds," Matthau said with a straight face, "and slice it thin."

At a dinner honoring the founder of Zabar's, a speaker said that his fortune was based on four words: "It's a little over."

The Gaiety Deli on West Forty-sixth Street was one of the best. Tiny, barely bigger than a phone booth, Milton Berle said it was doing so well that they were thinking of making the place smaller. When Eugene O'Neill's *The Iceman Cometh* opened on Broadway, it was in four long acts. After the first act there was an hour's meal break. During the run I recall the Gaiety, which was a block from the theater, featuring what they called an INTERMISHNOSH.

Marilyn Monroe, tasting her first matzo balls at the Stage Delicatessen, allegedly said, "Oh, they're absolutely delicious. What do they do with the rest of the matzo?"

As long as I'm recounting the apocryphal, Marilyn and Elizabeth Taylor were together in the powder room talking about Eddie Fisher when someone walked in. "Shh," Marilyn cautioned, "say it in Yiddish."

Sardi's was still the hub of the theater world's dining activities when the aging Sir Cedric Hardwicke was there with a beautiful young woman. While she went to powder her nose, a friend of Hardwicke's came over to the table.

"Say, old boy," he greeted Sir Cedric, "is she your semiannual?"

"No, dear boy, she's my annual-semi."

S. J. Perelman was telling Bob Hector, the book publisher, about a certain Hollywood writer who was the tightest man he'd ever known.

"I'll tell you how tight he is," said Perelman. "I once saw him just sit there at a table in Sardi's and watch as the quadriplegic he was having lunch with picked up the check with his teeth."

Which brings us back to the Russian Tea Room, socially the closest thing we have at lunch in New York to a Hollywood studio commissary. There was a time when such regulars as Anatole Chujoy, the editor of *Dance News,* the director Harold Clurman, the actress Olive Deering, her husband Leo Penn (Sean's father) and brother Alfred Ryder, were permanent fixtures in the prestigious front booths.

"Let's meet at the Tea Room," someone suggested.

"Where?"

"In front of Olive Deering."

Although it's been attributed to others, it was actually Olive who said after she had been working on Cecil B. De Mille's *Ten Commandments* on location in the Mojave desert for endless weeks, "Who do you have to sleep with to get *off* this picture?"

The greatest stir that has ever been created at lunch in the Tea Room, where luminaries in the arts are more or less taken for granted, was when Robby Lantz, the agent, walked in with his newest client, Joe Namath, who was seeking a career as an actor. Lantz is a cultured, European type who has never taken a particular interest in sports. Halfway through lunch the maître d' brought Lantz a note from Sam Cohn, a fellow agent.

"A football team," it read, *"has eleven men."*

Two writers were lunching one day and spotted Cohn, whom neither had seen for a long time, sitting in his usual booth at the Tea Room.

"My God!" one of them exclaimed. "Look at how much weight he's lost!" How, he wondered, did Sam, whose eccentricities include nibbling on Kleenex, do it?

"He must be eating diet Kleenex."

11

○●○○●○

Let's make a deal

○●○○●○

---○---

An agent and a client were on a backpacking trip in the High Sierras when suddenly they saw, barely twenty feet in front of them, a mountain lion ready to pounce. They froze. After a moment the agent, without saying a word, slipped off his backpack and put it on the ground. "You've got to be kidding," his client said, "You can't run faster than a mountain lion."

"I don't have to," the agent replied. "All I have to do is run faster than you."

---○---

TALENT AGENTS ARE a part of every facet of show business. Nothing gets done without them. The stories and jokes about agents are undoubtedly the most common and widely circulated in the business. In certain instances, as you will see, I have omitted their names to protect the guilty.

I have been with my agent, Abbey Greshler, almost from the beginning of my career, a record of sorts, no doubt. I have been accused of being a rather constant fellow, having had the same agent for thirty-five years, the same press agent, John Springer, for thirty years, the same voice teacher for thirty-two years, and the same wife, Florence, for longer.

Early in my career, before Greshler, I was with the William Morris office and nothing ever happened. I got my job in *Caesar and Cleopatra* on my own. I had run into someone on the street—A. Winfield Hoeny—an actor with an enormous voice. Hoeny told me to go down the block to the Empire Theatre, where Sam Wanamaker was casting people. I went and Wanamaker, who may have heard Hoeny from down the street, gave me a part. I then went to my agent at William Morris and asked him about *Caesar and Cleopatra.* He said, "Tony, there's nothing in it for you." And so I negotiated the contract myself and shortly thereafter left the Morris office.

○ 278 ○

I used to play paddleball every day at the Gotham Health Club with Joey Foreman, a comedian. He was always telling me jokes about Abbey Greshler. There were lots of jokes about Abbey, who I always assumed was a made-up character, the quintessential, stereotypical actors' agent. Foreman's Greshler joke that day went as follows: Greshler calls Sidney Piermont, the booker at the Paramount Theatre, and says "Sidney, I've got a great act for you. I just discovered this guy. Are you sitting down, Sidney? I found him in South America and believe me, Sidney, he's going to be the greatest act you've ever presented at the Paramount. The greatest. It's Adolf Hitler."

"Are you crazy, Abbey? He's the worst man who ever lived. He killed six million Jews."

"Sidney, the man made a few mistakes."

That night at *Inherit the Wind* an usher brought a note to me in my dressing room at intermission. *"Would like to meet with you after the show. Abbey Greshler."*

○ 279 ○

I thought it was Joey Foreman having some fun, but Ed Begley, who dressed with me, said, "No, no, Greshler's a well-known agent. He can do a lot for you." When Abbey came backstage, I saw before me the palest man I have ever seen. He still is. In fact he is sometimes referred to as an éminence grise. Tom Korman, another agent, started a rumor that when Ted Turner finishes colorizing the MGM film library (Herb Sargent says Turner is saving the first ten minutes of *Wizard of Oz* for last) Greshler will be next. Larry Gelbart says he recently saw Greshler at a party with his widow.

Greshler and I strolled up Broadway together that night and as we were passing the Paramount Theatre he said, "Sidney!" and he introduced me to Sidney Piermont, who until then I had always thought was a made-up character too. And here it is, thirty-five years later and I'm still with Abbey, who's famous for calling you up in the middle of the night.

"Tony, where are you?"

"I'm home in bed, Abbey."

○ 280 ○

"Are you going to be there in thirty minutes?"

"Yes."

"I'll call you back."

Shortly after Greshler became my agent, I signed a contract with Twentieth Century-Fox. They had exclusivity—I couldn't work for anyone else without their permission. But Abbey put a clause in my contract that gave me the right to do White Owl cigar commercials on television.

"Abbey, what's the matter with you? You must be crazy. You know I would never do a cigar commercial."

"Leave it in, leave it in," he said.

About a year later I wanted a big favor from Fox. Abbey and I went into Lew Schreiber's office together and asked the head of the studio to release me for a year to do a play. Schreiber turned us down.

"Lew," Abbey said, "you haven't seen this boy on TV with a White Owl cigar in his mouth, have you?"

Schreiber let me do the play.

○ 281 ○

A moment of glory almost came for Abbey, who has always wanted to be an actor, when Francis Ford Coppola considered using him for the Meyer Lansky part in *The Godfather.* Abbey came to the studio every day to rehearse with Jack Klugman, who is also his client, for the screen test. When he heard that Lee Strasberg got the part he made the typical actor's bitter complaint: "Coppola went for a name."

Perhaps it's less true of the newer breed, but ten-percenters, especially the vintage variety, are thought of as ruthless, unscrupulous, conniving, and heartless— and I'm speaking now of the agents who are considered the most reputable in the business. As he almost always did, Fred Allen probably put it best: "You can take all the integrity in Hollywood, put it in a flea's navel, and there'll still be room enough for two caraway seeds and the heart of an agent."

They tell a story about a Hollywood agent's young son who asked his father what the word *integrity* meant. "Let me give you an example, son. Let's say Kirk

Douglas sent me a check for the agency's commission on the new picture we got for him. And let's say a few days later his business manager sends me another check in error for the same commission. Integrity is whether or not I tell my partner.''

With the exception of my own, of course, agents are necessary evils, the butts of a lot of jokes. People seem to think they're some subspecies who are immune from all the laws of morality. An agent is expected to lie and it is perfectly acceptable because he's doing it not for himself but on behalf of someone else—a client. An agent is an employment agent, after all. If you're hiring a secretary or a maid, let's say, and you ask the employment agency if he or she is reliable or whatever, what are they going to tell you—''Yes, she's been fired from every job because of drunkenness''? Of course not. And lying is what Abbey has done for all his clients, including me.

As we were about to start negotiating a deal on a new picture, Abbey told me,

○ 283 ○

"The one thing an agent can't lie about is his client's last salary."

"But then," I asked, "how come you lied about the salary I got on the picture I did last month?"

"That was different."

Back in the McCarthy-blacklist days, I was signed to do a great big TV special for, as I recall, the fiftieth anniversary of Chevrolet or something like that. The host was James Arness, whose company was also producing the show. I was already in rehearsal when they sent a loyalty oath over to Abbey's office. He just sent it back. They called and asked why he had returned it without my signature and Abbey said, "Because Tony just won't sign a loyalty oath." "Why not?" "Because," Abbey said straight-faced, "he's a communist." They said, "Oh," and that was the end of it. They never said another word and Arness, who was farther to the right than his mentor, John Wayne, couldn't have been nicer to me on the set.

To an agent the deal is everything.

○ 284 ○

Two agents who had both seen much better days ran into each other on Broadway.

"The Salmaggi Circus is folding."

"I heard."

"They're selling an Indian elephant for $150. Are you interested?"

"Waddya, crazy? I got two small rooms on West 49th Street."

"They'll throw in a second elephant for forty bucks."

"Now you're talking!"

In Hollywood the deal overrides all other considerations. So important, in fact, is the deal that most studios now are not run by picture makers, unfortunately, but by former agents. The deal is often far more creative than any of the other elements of a picture—the package, as it's known. The day may be fast approaching in Hollywood when instead of the often puerile screenplays, they'll be shooting the far more creative deals.

Agents have been known not to read the books and screenplays they represent. Why, some ask, let reality dampen their enthusiasm?

○ 285 ○

Alan Jay Lerner once sent his agent a new screenplay, all the middle pages of which he had glued together. The script was returned to him in the same condition. When Lerner asked his agent what he thought of the script, he said, "Kid, it's the best thing you've ever done."

A powerhouse agent was trying to get Jack Warner to buy a client's novel. He was asking for what is now referred to in the industry as "megabucks."

"It'll make a great film, Jack. It's one helluva yarn, believe me."

"You've read it?" the dubious Warner asked.

"Of course I have."

"All right, I'll tell you what," Warner said. "If you can tell me how it ends, it's a deal."

One of the things I find most amusing about agents is how fast they are on their feet. They're always prepared to go in whatever direction necessary.

"If you don't agree with what I'm saying," an agent said to Larry Gelbart, "then it isn't necessarily what I mean."

Agents—the good ones—are, above all else, indefatigable. Producer-director Stanley Kramer ran into agent Marty Baum.

"Marty, you're just the guy who can help me. Do you remember that character actor—short, kind of fat, bushy black eyebrows, always wore a derby? I can't remember his name."

"You mean Eddie Brophy?"

"That's it! I've got a part for him in my new movie—*It's a Mad Mad Mad Mad World.* Do you happen to know where I can find him?"

"Of course I do," said Baum, "I'm his agent."

Then and there Kramer and Baum negotiated a deal—a very rich one—for Brophy's services. Baum then went back to his office and told his secretary to drop everything.

"Find Eddie Brophy!"

Not only didn't Baum have any idea where Brophy was but he didn't represent him.

After a couple of days the secretary

found a number for Brophy. The actor's wife answered the phone and Baum told her that he had just negotiated a deal for her husband to work in the new Stanley Kramer picture.

"But Mr. Baum, Eddie's been dead for three years."

Baum called Kramer and told him the bad news.

"Marty, do you mean to say you sold me a dead actor?"

"You bought him from me, didn't you?"

"Gulf coast shrimps are the best," said a guest on the Johnny Carson show. Groucho, who was also a guest that night, said, "Have you tried the shrimps at the Morris office?"

George Jessel called his daughter in California from New York where it was snowing.

"The snowflakes are falling right outside my window, darling."

"How big are they, Daddy?"

"Bigger than anyone in the William Morris office."

Short has always been a tradition at William Morris, the world's largest talent agency. Abe Lastfogel, who was barely five feet tall, ran the agency and was one of the most powerful men in Hollywood. Lastfogel was referred to around the office as "Big Abe." At a Christmas office party an agent on his way up within the hierarchy introduced his young son to Lastfogel. His son's ambition in life, he told his boss, was to be an agent.

"And, Abe, he's only twelve and look how short he is already."

The producer Walter Wanger discovered that his wife, the beautiful screen star Joan Bennett, was having an affair with Jennings Lang, one of those rarities among agents—he is very tall. The irate producer caught up with Lang in a parking lot and shot him in the testicles.

"It's a good thing it wasn't a William Morris agent," said screenwriter Harry Kurnitz, "or the bullet would have hit him right between the eyes."

Lastfogel often went across the street to sun himself on a rubber float in the pool of the Beverly Wilshire Hotel. More than one deal was consummated in the middle of that pool by people who swam out to negotiate with Abe. Even Abbey, who can't swim at all, managed to get to Lastfogel when he drifted down to the shallow end.

Lastfogel asked one of his agency's clients, Ben Gazzara, the actor, what he was doing next.

"I'm doing a play on Broadway. It's Anouilh."

"Better a newy than an oldie," Lastfogel commented.

Walter Bernstein, a screenwriter blacklisted during the McCarthy era, could not work at Paramount Pictures unless he agreed to send them a letter clearing himself of any and all involvements in communist front organizations. This, as a matter of principle, he refused to do.

"Don't worry about it," said his agent, who was short enough to be an agent at William Morris but had his own office, "I'll speak to Y. Frank Freeman, the head of the studio. I promise you that you're not going to have to write that letter. It's outrageous that they would ask you to do such a thing. It's offensive, un-principled, unethical, un-American, and a moral outrage. As long as I am your agent, you have my personal guarantee that you will never have to write a letter like that. Never!"

The agent called Freeman in Bernstein's presence and stated his position very clearly and forcefully. And then he listened, and listened, and listened. He then said good-bye and hung up.

"Walter," the agent said, "write the god-damned letter."

Producer Sidney Beckerman, poolside at the Beverly Hills Hotel, was on the phone with super-agent Sam Cohn, who was in his New York office. Beckerman was trying to wrap up the movie rights to the hit Broadway musical *Cabaret*. I'm not sure of the numbers but the negotiation, which, as they say, was down to the short strokes, went something like this:

"You're going to have to pay more money up front," said Cohn, who was representing the show's producer, Hal Prince.

"How about one million?"

"Hold on while I check that with Hal," said Cohn. "I've got him on the other line."

Beckerman waited.

"Hal says he'll come down to a million six."

"I'll give him a million five," said Beckerman, "and that's my last offer."

"Hold on."

Beckerman waited a few minutes.

"Okay, Sidney," Cohn said, "it's a deal."

Beckerman was thrilled.

"Please tell Hal how happy I am and thank him for me."

"Thank him yourself," Cohn said. "He's sitting on the other side of the pool."

During the Korean War, when Douglas MacArthur was summarily cashiered by President Truman, the five-star general returned to the States and made his "old soldiers never die, they just fade away" speech to a joint session of Congress. One of agent Robby Lantz's clients, who had watched the speech on television, expressed his disgust.

"Have you ever heard anyone so pompous, so arrogant, so ridiculous?" the actor fumed.

"Well," said Lantz, who looks at life the way all of us do in show business, "you must remember he's done very little television."

Perhaps the most famous of all agent stories is the one about John Wayne, who had a dispute with his agent and decided to leave him. He picked another agent at random, called him, and said he wanted to be represented by him.

"Draw up the papers and I'll come to your office on Saturday morning to sign them."

The struggling agent couldn't believe his good fortune. Saturday morning Wayne walked in as he said he would. He went over the papers in silence and, just

○ 293 ○

as he was about to sign them, looked up and said, "Are you Jewish?"

"Not necessarily."

The story that for me best exemplifies an agent's mentality is one about Kurt Frings. Once a powerful Hollywood agent, Kurt and his wife, Ketti, who wrote the successful Broadway play *Look Homeward, Angel,* based on the Thomas Wolfe novel, originally came to this country as refugees from Germany. (The movie *Hold Back the Dawn,* starring Charles Boyer and Olivia de Havilland, was a dramatization of their flight across the Mexican border into California.)

When they arrived in Hollywood, Frings went to work as a valet parking attendant at Chasen's restaurant. At the end of every day he was paid five dollars. The next morning he would take the $5 bill to a bank, where he had it changed for five singles. He'd then take the five singles to another bank where he had them changed into twenty quarters.

Frings was asked why in the world he

did this every day and he replied, "Because sooner or later someone is going to make a mistake, and I can assure you it's not going to be me."

○●○○●○

The

space

race

○●○○●○

---○---

When Florenz Ziegfeld arrived in Chicago for the opening of one of his musical extravaganzas, not a single member of the press was at the train station to greet him. He sent the following telegram to his press agent: THANKS FOR SNEAKING ME INTO TOWN.

---○---

PRESS AGENTS, for those who aren't quite certain, are the men and women who are paid to use their often considerable skills, wiles, and ingenuity to get their clients—be they corporate or individuals—free space and time in the print, radio, and television media. In all the years Mike and I have known each other, the only time we've worked together was in the early sixties when he was the supervising publicity man on all of Warner Bros.' European productions. It was on the lovely but barren Greek island of Hydra on an unmemorable picture that is best left that way—forgotten.

There are some who think they can build their careers through publicity and there are people who are famous for being famous. The reason for having a press agent, at least for me, is not to get on television talk shows or see my name in the newspapers or magazines as often as possible but to protect me and serve as a buffer between me and the media people. I will not submit to personal publicity. There's only one thing the public knows about me: I don't smoke.

In my opinion the only legitimate publicity is that which sells—promotes—your movie, play, book, or whatever. Then the publicity is justified and it must be orchestrated by someone who knows what he's doing. But the publicity department for, let's say, that movie or play will book you on any radio or television show, schedule you for as many newspaper and magazine interviews as they can. That's their job. So your own personal press

agent has to protect you, screen all the re-
quests that come in—as many as thirty or
forty a week—for meaningless interviews,
appearances at benefits, supermarket
openings, showing up at this or that. I'm
one of those guys who can't say no. I've
always needed someone to say no for me.

John Springer and I first met when I
was under contract to Fox and he worked
in their publicity department. Springer
chooses the things that are worthwhile.
He's the reason I'm the president of the
Myasthenia Gravis Foundation, as a matter of fact. Almost anybody in the New
York or Los Angeles area who's giving any
kind of charity event calls the various personal press agents or, in the old days, the
studio publicity departments, to get someone—a star—to show up. And press
agents always try to cooperate for the sake
of charity. One day Springer called me
and said there's something called myasthenia gravis and they're giving a banquet
and would I show up. So I did. And I got
very interested. That was twenty years
ago and since then I've devoted a large

part of my life to myasthenia gravis, a wasting neuromuscular disease whose cause is unknown and whose cure is undiscovered.

When you were under contract to a studio, as I was, you were at the beck and call of the publicity department. Some guy who had invented a kind of rocket motor that you could strap on yourself and travel around in the air wanted me to put it on and soar out over the freeway and land somewhere. It would be a great publicity story for the contraption and for me. Someone in the publicity department at Fox actually asked me to do it and I was dumb and young enough to think it might be fun. Thank God for Abbey Greshler, who said, "Over my dead body are you going to strap that thing around yourself and fly over the freeway." And that was the end of it.

When Eva Marie Saint, who's my dearest and oldest friend in this business, made it big in *On the Waterfront,* the publicity department of Columbia wanted her to go everywhere to promote the movie.

And she said, "Yes, I'll go on Steve Allen, yes, I'll go on Ernie Kovacs—but I will not go down to Philadelphia at five o'clock in the morning to appear on some talk show that originates in some cafeteria over station WSHIT." The head of the department was indignant. "If you think making movies consists solely of coming to the studio and putting on your makeup and acting in front of the cameras, you're wrong. If you don't want to go out and promote that picture, then you ain't got any talent!" That is as good an expression of a publicity man's credo as I have ever heard.

Sometimes press agents will go to the most extraordinary lengths to publicize pictures. When Mike was working on Laurence Olivier's truly magnificent film of *Richard III,* he got what he thought was a sound idea. There are two historical interpretations of Richard: the evil Plantagenet monarch, according to Shakespeare, who lived under Elizabeth, a Tudor, and a benign king as depicted in Josephine Tey's historically revisionist novel *Daughter of Time,* which *The New York Times* has called the best mystery ever written. Why not commission Salvador Dali to do a double portrait of Olivier, as he had done of his wife, Gala? Mike went to his boss, who told him to proceed. He made an appointment to see Dali at the St. Regis Hotel, where the flamboyant artist always stayed when he was in New York. Mike rang the bell of his suite, the door opened, and there stood Dali, his unmistakable waxed black moustache curled diabolically upward at both ends. They made small talk in the living room for a few minutes before Mike mustered the courage to tell the great surrealist painter why he had come to see him. Would he, Mike asked—very reticently lest he offend— consider doing a double portrait of Laurence Olivier as an evil and benevolent Richard III?

Without hesitating for a moment Dali popped up out of his chair, crossed the room, picked up two empty frames, and said, "What size: $25,000 or $15,000?"

The first of the many pictures Mike worked on abroad was as the publicist for

Sir Carol Reed's *The Man Between.* Before he left New York to join the production on location in West Berlin, Alfred Katz, a fellow publicist, asked him if he could arrange to have the film's star, James Mason, present the city's mayor, Ernst Reuter, with a check for $100,000 on behalf of Katz's client the International Rescue Committee.

As soon as Mike arrived in Berlin, he made all of the necessary arrangements with Mason and the mayor's press officer. However, on the day of the scheduled occasion, the check from the IRC had still not arrived. Undaunted, Mike wrote out a check to Mayor Reuter for $100,000 on one of his own personal checks—the ten-cents-a-check, $100 minimum-balance variety—and signed it Rear Admiral Richard E. Byrd, who was the head of the IRC. Mike explained what he had done to both Mason and Reuter in the mayor's office before they walked into an adjoining conference room in which were gathered more journalists than Mike had ever seen in one place before: newspapers, wire services, news magazines, photographers, radio reporters, and a battery of newsreel cameras. This, to the delight of Mike's press-agent's heart, was to be a major news event. James Mason presented the check to Mayor Reuter as flashbulbs popped and newsreel cameras turned. It was a publicist's dream come true until one of the newsreel cameramen, more thorough than the others, asked Mason to hold the check so he could shoot it in close-up.

While the insert was being filmed, the very distinguished mayor, standing off to one side, whispered to Mike in a conspiratorial tone, "Now ve vill bose go to jail."

The ballet is one of the enthusiasms Mike and I share. When he was doing the publicity for the Ballets Russes de Monte Carlo, he got a call from *Cosmopolitan* magazine. They were researching an article on dancers who began taking dance lessons for therapeutic reasons. They wanted to know if the English prima ballerina Alicia Markova had had infantile paralysis as a child. Mike said he would ask her.

He called Markova's apartment and her sister Doris answered. Alicia was out. Mike asked Doris if Alicia, who is, I believe, about a year older, ever had polio when she was a child. "I really don't recall," said Doris, "but I shall ask Alicia when she comes in. She has a very good memory for that sort of thing."

Press agents are often more colorful and interesting than their clients. Irving Hoffman and Jack Tirman are two examples that come to mind.

Time magazine was preparing a cover story on Tallulah Bankhead in its customary meticulous fashion. A researcher assigned to the story was interviewing the actress's press agent, Irving Hoffman. *Time* wanted to know just how accurate all the rumors were about Bankhead's sexual escapades. Hoffman was being very guarded.

"For instance," the researcher pressed on, "have you ever made it with her?"

"She'll kill me if she ever hears I said it," said Hoffman, lowering his voice, "but the answer is no."

Jack Tirman, a very Runyonesque personality, was publicizing *Godzilla,* the first of the Japanese monster pictures.

"How, for instance, does Godzilla compare to King Kong?" he was asked by a member of the press.

"Godzilla," said Tirman, "makes King Kong look like a faggot."

The complicated machinations of press agents, let me assure you, don't always work. Tirman was in the New York office of Warner Bros. publicizing the Cole Porter biographical film *Night and Day.* He suggested to the head of publicity, Larry Golub, at a department brainstorming session, that they rent an English bulldog, the mascot of Yale University, where Porter had gone to college; put the dog in a blue dog blanket with a white *Y* on it; and take pictures of the animal at the theater's box office with the first tickets to the movie clenched between its teeth. Farfetched though it was, Golub approved. But not one newspaper or magazine anywhere in the country ran a picture of the stunt. Golub, a stern taskmaster, demanded an explanation. Tirman ran through a series of excuses, one lamer than the next. Golub wasn't buying any of them. Finally, in desperation, Tirman said, "And besides, Larry, I've never seen such an ugly dog!"

A few years back, in the days of the nickel phone call, Tirman, never the most patient of men, called his office from a pay phone. His young part-time assistant, Marty Ragaway, who became a successful comedy writer and whom I mentioned in a previous chapter, answered. Ragaway was a stammerer. Later that day, when Tirman got back to his office, he took Ragaway aside, put his arm around him, and said, "Kid, do me a favor. Don't answer the phone anymore when I call. By the time you say hello, it's cost me ten cents."

Tirman on the phone with his wife: "Fawn, it's such a beautiful day, why don't you take the subway uptown and go to a movie?"

The accepted wisdom among Broadway press agents, I'm told, was that if you called columnist Earl Wilson with a funny story he might not get it. Your chances of breaking the column with an amusing item about a client were enhanced considerably if you gave it to his assistant, Martin Burden, who had a much better sense of humor. One day Tirman called the Wilson office with a funny item and heard Earl say hello. Tirman hung up immediately and then started to worry.

"Gee," he said to his secretary, "do you think Earl knew it was me?"

Lee Solters is another very colorful, rather Runyonesque press agent. He's based on the West Coast now and I see him from time to time at Nate-n-Al's, where he's one of the regulars at breakfast. When Solters was publicizing *The Trials of O'Brien,* a TV series starring Peter Falk, he got Peter a two-page photo layout and story in the Sunday magazine section of the New York *Daily News.* But Bud Austin, the head of television for Filmways, the show's producer, had been told that Falk would also be on the cover.

"Bud," Solters said, "there was nothing I could do. There are two people who Ben Handel, the magazine section's editor, refuses to put on the cover: Sammy Davis, Jr., and Peter Falk."

"Why's that, Lee?"

"Because they both have glass eyes."

"Couldn't you have gotten Peter on the cover winking?"

Solters, who was once quite rotund, was getting into one of New York's new compact cabs with Walter Slezak, the very portly star of the hit Broadway musical *Fanny*.

"Where can I take you?" asked the cabbie.

"To a larger taxi," Solters replied.

Very shortly after World War II had ended, a client of Solters's said he was going to Europe.

"But why go now?" Solters asked. "It's still so devastated."

"Because I want to see Europe before it closes."

As the clouds of World War II were gathering, the morale in the advertising and publicity department at Warner Bros. was very low, its productivity declining. Many on the staff were of draft age. Charley Einfeld, the department head, decided to have a meeting at the end of the week to boost everyone's spirits.

"Men," Einfeld began the meeting on Friday, December 5, 1941, "you have my personal guarantee that there will be no war."

13

On the air!

Bartlett Robinson, a regular on Young Widder Brown, *a daytime soap that was done live on radio, was supposed to say, "I've come to call on Mary," but he reversed it. That was the end of that day's episode.*

A FTER I GRADUATED from the Neighborhood Playhouse I began making the rounds, going from ad agency to ad agency—they controlled the shows in those days—looking for work in radio. Diligence: that was the secret of not being unemployed—and ninety percent of all actors were out of work ninety percent of the time. That's still true. I'm the only exception I know of—I was never out of work. There were a lot of shows originating in New York then—soaps and dramas.

They were on all three networks all day and night long: "Live from New York . . ."

Radio was what subsidized a lot of us while we looked for work in the theater. It didn't pay well, but if you did enough shows you made a living. A fifteen-minute sponsored show paid thirty-three dollars. An unsponsored fifteen-minute show paid, I believe, twenty-four dollars. The big evening shows—the half hours and hours—paid much better. And, in those days before tape, you did them twice. Once, let's say, at nine in the evening, and then again at midnight for the West Coast. The really successful radio actors were working from morning to night. Ed Begley told me that in his first year in New York he did more than two thousand radio shows.

All of us would run into each other every day at our hangouts: Walgreen's Drugstore in the Paramount Building on Broadway, Colby's in the CBS building, and the actors' lounge on the third floor of the RCA building. Sometimes you'd see the big radio actors sitting there—Myron McCormick, Ken Roberts, Gary Merrill, Joe Di Santis, Everett Sloane, Hans Conried, Paul Stewart—but mostly they were too busy working. There was a direct line at NBC to all the phone services we used— Radio Registry and Lexington were the two most popular. When you were called for a job—in radio and theater—they always reached you through your service. You'd check in with them throughout the day and very often they'd track you down and have you paged. There was a famous radio actor—Raymond Edward Johnson— who got a part playing Thomas Jefferson in Sidney Kingsley's play *The Patriots.* Opening night, as he was standing in the wings waiting to go on, the doorman came to him and said, "Radio Registry is calling you."

The same guys I'd seen before I left for the Army were still sitting in the NBC lounge when I came back four years later. When I toured in 1947 with Cornell in *Barretts,* we played the Biltmore Theater in Hollywood. I hopped a streetcar and found my way to Schwab's on Sunset, an actors' hangout, and there, standing in front of the drugstore, was Lenny Bremer, one of the same guys who was always in the lounge at NBC. I didn't get to Hollywood again for another seven years with *Mr. Peepers,* which NBC tried to get us to shoot out there. I passed Schwab's and there was Bremer standing exactly where I had left him. I didn't come to Hollywood again until 1957 when I made *Oh Men! Oh Women!* and there was my friend Lenny, still standing in front of the drugstore. Schwab's finally went out of business a couple of years ago. And so did Lenny. He died.

Sorry to tell you this, but I did not love radio. I never felt that radio acting was acting. And I didn't enjoy the gags actors played on one another. The object was always to break someone up while on the air live. I remember a fellow actor, Luis Van Rooten, once wrote something on the back of his script and held it up in front of me:

YOU'RE FIRED!

Another prank was to set fire to an actor's script as he stood at the mike reading it.

That, I'm sorry to say, was typical of the level of the jokes. That, and lower.

An announcer, all alone in front of a live mike, reading the news for about fifteen minutes, was the most inviting and vulnerable target of all. Guys would do almost anything to break him up. One standard prank was to stand in front of the table the announcer was seated at and take your cock out. The announcer always tried his damnedest not to look up because if he broke up—and there were plenty of times when he did—there'd be fifteen minutes of airtime to fill.

One day, a guy with his cock out wasn't getting the announcer's attention, and so he put it on the table. Without looking up the announcer slammed it with his fist as hard as he could. It hurts to get your cock slammed like that.

Lowell Thomas was one of radio's

○ 319 ○

legendary breaker-uppers, from all accounts a very easy mark. At least once a
year he could be relied on to go to pieces
on his nightly newscast, which was an
American institution. He always ended the
show with a human-interest story before
signing off with "And so long until tomorrow," his trademark. Whatever the feature
story was, Thomas would always read it
cold. That evening's feature was about a
prize dog that was being shipped across
country in a cage by Railway Express. The
dog managed to get out of the cage at
some railroad siding and they caught him,
put him back in the cage, and slammed
the door shut, cutting off his tail. The
dog's owner sued Railway Express and,
the story ended, "He collected $35,000,
which is an awful lot of money for a piece
of tail." Thomas realized what he had
said. It was the end of the show and he
fell on the floor, laughing, unable to say,
"And so long until tomorrow." Helpless,
Thomas looked into the control booth but
couldn't see anyone. The director, pro-

ducer, and all the technicians were also on the floor, laughing hysterically.

The next evening Thomas began his show with an apology.

"Ladies and gentlemen, yesterday I did something very unprofessional and I wish to apologize for it. It will not happen again." He then went into the news portion of the show. "Today, the British ambassador to the Soviet Union, Sir Stifford Crapps . . ." And that was as far as he got. The studio organist had to play almost fifteen minutes of music. The following day Thomas began with an apology for his spoonerism of the night before and his assurance that it would never happen again. "Of course," he continued, "the name that gave me so much trouble yesterday was Sir Stifford Crapps . . ." and once again that evening's newscast was filled with almost fifteen minutes of organ music.

A very old actor, Julian Noah, had only one line on some soap opera or other and it came out "Oh, poppycack. Cock. Cack!"

What makes these gaffes even funnier is that an actor often does not realize what he's done. You stand there trying to figure out why everyone around you has gone to pieces. The expression of utter consternation on your face makes them laugh that much harder.

Live television—especially dramas—could be a nightmare. David Niven once told me that if I ever saw him on live TV it would be safe for me to assume that he was in terrible trouble financially. He swore off live TV after his last *Playhouse 90.* There was always an enormous amount of pressure on all of those live television dramas. David, as he almost always did, took it upon himself to relieve the tension. Minutes before airtime he sauntered out of his dressing room in his shirt and tie but without his trousers on. He paraded around the studio and everyone in the cast and crew laughed. It was the very thing that was needed. As Niven heard the announcer say, "Ladies and gentlemen, welcome to *Playhouse 90* . . ." or whatever those introductory words used to be, he sauntered back to his dressing room to put on the rest of his clothes. Only, he had locked himself out! The stagehands had to use an ax to break through the fireproof door into the dressing room. The sound of metal being chopped reverberated through the land that night. The usually unflappable Niven never recovered, nor did anyone else. The show—all ninety minutes of it—was a shambles.

Sidney Lumet was rehearsing *The Dybbuk* for live television, and as airtime was rapidly approaching, Lumet still didn't have a timing. He gathered the cast and crew together and told them that he wanted a run-through and that they were not to stop for anything. All was going smoothly until they got to the scene when the Grand Rabbi, portrayed by an actor from Israel's Habimah Theatre, surrounded by his young rabbinical assistants, all of them bearded and dressed in their Hasidic black hats and coats, said in his heavily accented, stentorian-toned English, "And we shall go to the cemetery at the dark of midnight where we shall exorcise the Dybbuk! . . ." At this point Gene Saks, who was playing one of the young rabbis, made an unscheduled interruption.

"Uh-uh," said Saks, rolling his eyes and doing his best imitation of Stepin Fetchit, the famous black screen comedian, "not me, boss."

That put an end to the run-through for about fifteen minutes while everyone but the bewildered actor from Israel got hysterical.

We did *Mr. Peepers* live every week, thirty-nine weeks a year. It was Wally Cox's first acting job and it made him a star. Wally's friends—people like Marlon Brando and Maureen Stapleton—were always making Wally perform his hilarious monologues in living rooms. When enough of us told him often enough that he really should be a professional performer, he decided to do something about it. Someone in the group knew Barney Josephson, who had a nightclub, and Wally went on. Fred Coe came to see him and signed him for Talent Associates and NBC, who were contractually obligated to come up with a vehicle for him. And that was the genesis of *Mr. Peepers.* Wally never really liked acting. He probably would have been much happier if he had remained a silversmith.

We never would get an accurate timing until the dress rehearsals, most of which didn't end until about fifteen minutes before we went on the air. Whenever we were over they always gave the cuts to me. They couldn't give them to Marion Lorne, whose whole act was stammering —"daba daba daba, er . . ." There just wasn't any point in giving them to her. And Wally was always so vague that he just sort of floated through his scenes, never that specific about his lines. And so the director, Hal Keith, always gave the cuts to me—"In the first scene you cut the first two lines, in the second scene come in after instead of before, in the third scene cut out your whole big speech." I'd get all of these cuts just before we went on the air. There were no cue cards to help me. Keith would always say to me—it became a ritual, a running gag between us—"I hate to take these lines away from you, but you just couldn't handle them."

Wally was completely self-taught. He had to learn something about acting along the way. His instincts were very good. He never made a mistake. He learned how to do it right from the word go—just by observing.

Wally and I were driving somewhere or other and a cop stopped us. I've never seen anyone get so nervous. Wally's lips were trembling, his hands shook, and his voice croaked. The cop let him go.

"Gee, Wally," I said, "how did you do it?"

"I turned on my cowardice."

I don't know why, but whenever the phone rang at rehearsals, I'd pick it up. Frequently it was Jim Fritzell, who, with his partner, Everett Greenbaum, were the head writers. When Jim heard my voice, he'd whisper, "How's your cock?" It always broke me up. It always caught me by surprise and I'd slide down the wall, giggling helplessly. I couldn't contain myself and what made it even worse is I'd have to try to stifle my laughter because they were rehearsing. Jim knew I couldn't take it and he wrote a whole episode around it. He had Wally buy a car and five times during the show I had to say, "How's your car?" This was live television and Jim knew he had me in his power.

Burt Shevelove, who also worked a lot for Talent Associates, had an assistant he couldn't stand, mostly because she was so efficient. "As I was yelling at Tom Poston about something," Burt told me, "I heard her on the phone ordering flowers to be sent to Tom with a note from me: *'Sorry, baby, I lost my head.'* "

The five years I spent working on the television version of *The Odd Couple* were mostly a very happy, enjoyable experience for me. Felix Unger, the character I played, is based on Danny Simon, Neil Simon's older brother. In fact, the entire situation—two opposites living together— is something Danny actually lived for a while after his divorce. Danny began writing it as a play, gave up on it, and gave the idea to Neil. The rest, as they say, is theatrical history.

One of the questions I'm asked in life that annoys me most is "Are you like Felix?" No, I'm not. And I'm nothing like Danny Simon, the original, whom I know well. And, he's nothing like Felix.

It can't be very easy being the older brother of anyone as gifted and successful as Neil Simon. Danny was once introduced by his mother to her card-playing cronies as "my son's brother." What's especially revealing about that story is that Danny made it up.

But Neil always acknowledges how much he learned from Danny about comedy writing. So, for that matter, does Woody Allen.

Danny hasn't changed very much over the years. Just before Mike came back to live in New York after twelve years in Hollywood, he got a call from Danny. Years ago Danny, Neil, and Mike were all office boys together at Warner Bros. in

New York and they've been friends ever since.

"Danny," Mike said, "I'm moving back to New York."

"Give me your address and phone number. I'll call you when I'm there."

Mike gave Danny his address, which included his apartment number, 3DA.

"What do you mean, 3DA?"

"What do you mean, what do I mean? It's apartment 3DA."

"But that's ridiculous," Danny said. "I've never heard of an apartment with a number and two letters."

"Danny," Mike said, "are you rewriting my apartment?"

"It should either be D or A," Danny went on, undaunted.

"How's the 3?"

"The 3's fine, but it should be 3D or 3A."

"Danny," Mike said, not knowing how else to end the nonsensical discussion, "let me think about it and I'll call you back, okay?"

○ 329 ○

Just before Mike left, Danny called him again.

"I know this is crazy, but I've lost Neil's phone number in New York and I've got to reach him. Would you please give it to me?"

"Okay, Danny I'll give it to you," Mike said, "but if you tell him where you got it, I'll kill you!"

Even though our careers have intertwined, I really don't know Neil Simon very well. I was renting a car in New York and Neil was standing next to me. His driver's license was on the counter and I saw his name: Marvin Neil Simon.

"Aha," I said, "so your first name is Marvin, is it?"

"Yes," he replied, "and now that you know, you must die."

When we were nearing the start date of the television version of *The Odd Couple,* we still hadn't found our Oscar Madison. The part had been offered to Jack Klugman, but he at first turned it down. We were sitting around racking our brains for casting ideas when Milton Goldman, the agent, said, "I've got it! Shelley Winters!"

In the show's opening credits you can see me walking up Fifth Avenue as Felix with two suitcases, on my way to Oscar's. The bags are awfully heavy and I put them down on the sidewalk and sit. A guy who was passing stopped and tried to help me with the bags. "Hey, are you okay, buddy?" He didn't know who I was, or that we were filming. He just wanted to help me. He nearly ruined the take. Ordinarily you can drop dead on the streets of New York and no one's going to help you. We kept it in the main titles. Another time we were shooting on the streets of New York and Otto Preminger walked through the shot. So we said to him, "If you sign a release, you can be in our television show." Preminger roared, "Do you want a lawsuit?" So we had to do a retake.

In the end credits there was a card that read MR. RANDALL'S AND MR. KLUGMAN'S WARDROBE BY WORSTED-TEX, a popular clothing line which was not really very fine and certainly not elegant enough for Jack and me. Worsted-Tex paid one of Holly-wood's finest tailors to make six suits for each of us every year—twelve suits in all —and they put the Worsted-Tex label in them. I'm still wearing them. So is Abbey Greshler. He's Jack's agent as well as mine, so his yearly ten percent commission on twelve suits was one suit with two pair of pants.

Of course, there were problems on *The Odd Couple* from time to time. Jerry Davis, the show's producer, said the fun-niest thing that was said during the years we all spent together on the show. Com-edy shows occasionally sell scripts to each other. Only once did I ever refuse to do a script. There were many times when I threatened to, but I always allowed myself to be talked back into it. With the writing staff we had—Garry Marshall, Jerry Bel-son, Harvey Miller—it was always reason-able to assume that the script could be fixed. The scripts were never really that good at the first readings anyway. But this particular script was impossible and I said, "We're not going to do it."

"We've got to do it, Tony," Jerry said. "I've spent $5000 on it. And besides which, it's good—very good."

"It's not good," I said.

"We'll make it good."

"It's no good and I'm not going to do it, Jerry."

"Well, what am I going to do with it?"

"Sell it to another show," I said.

"But who'd buy a piece of shit like this?"

We shot *The Odd Couple* in front of an audience with what is known as the three-camera technique—so called, I believe, because it employs three cameras. After the audience left each Friday night, we would dismiss two of the three camera crews and shoot a few pickup shots— shots we were unable to get during the show. One, I remember, took an hour to set up. It involved a leaking pipe dripping on Bartlett Robinson's bald head. During the show the actor had merely acted it. It was fine and the audience laughed. But the director wanted to show it and so a real pipe had to be rigged and the water

had to drip—not too fast, not too slow—
and it had to be lighted. The actor stood
there for an entire hour while the drops
fell and the director was satisfied that the
drops fell on exactly the right spot. Then
the cameraman was called in to shoot it.
He looked through his finder and said to
the actor, "Move six inches to your right."
He was bothered by a picture on the wall
in the background that was framing the
actor's head asymmetrically. We tried to
explain the purpose of the shot but that
meant nothing to him. More time was
spent arguing. He was angry but he gave
in and ordered the picture moved. Finally
it was settled when the script girl suggested the camera move six inches to the
left.

In Hollywood until quite recently, it
was most unusual to see a young cameraman. Almost every cameraman and his
crew had white hair. They were all old-
timers, most of whom went back to silent
films—in fact some of them would actually refer to your lines as titles. They'd say,
"When you hit this mark, then say your

title, then move to your next mark. . . ."
When we were doing the *Tony Randall
Show* on TV, we had one of these wonderful veterans, who took me aside one day
and said, "You're the best I've ever seen." I
was speechless with pride and modesty.
"You always hit your marks."

On TV variety shows, like Milton
Berle's, the next week's guest was usually
not set until the last minute; so in rehearsal Milton would announce: "Next
week—Irving Tishman!" It became a tradition. When I was moving into a new
apartment in New York, I wanted an unlisted number and the phone company
said there would be a $6 monthly charge
for it. So I told them to list the number in
the name of Irving Tishman. But they already had quite a few Irving Tishmans
and so I changed it to Ervine W. Tischman
and it was so listed for many years. I had
the happy delusion that I was besting the
phone company.

Dave Tebet, a very personable and lik-
able fellow, and someone who can get
things done, was for years NBC's liaison

with certain shows. Dave had a barber in New York who wanted to move to Los Angeles with his family. Dave called his friend Sammy Cahn, the songwriter, on the West Coast and asked him what he could do to get him a barber's license.

"It's as good as done," Cahn said. "Have him pack and move out."

The barber did just that, but after he had been in Hollywood for more than a month and a half, he still did not have his license.

"Mr. Cahn, I'm not like you and Mr. Tebet, you know. I don't have very much money. I've got to work. I have a family to feed."

Cahn called his lawyer, who was with one of Hollywood's most prestigious firms.

"I still haven't heard from Pat Brown, Sammy. Maybe you should call him. I know he'd love to hear from you."

Cahn called his friend Pat Brown, the governor of California.

"I'm doing everything I can, Sammy, but it's a lot tougher than I thought it would be. There are lots of problems—the unions. . . ."

"Say," Brown said after pausing for a few moments, "how would he like to be a judge?"

A long time ago I was a guest on the Jack Paar show—the Carson show's predecessor—when it was being done in New York live. The show went on the air at 11:15, after the late news, and lasted until one in the morning. On this particular night one of Paar's guests was a little fuzzy old man—not a performer—who came on with this extraordinary dog who looked just like him. The dog seemed to understand every word the man said. It was remarkable. He'd say, "In the sixth row, four seats in, there's a young woman wearing a plaid skirt. Go to her." And damned if the dog didn't go straight to her. Then he said, pointing to a microphone on a boom, "Find another one of these." The dog went straight to a microphone on a stand. Uncanny! Jack Paar said, "Tell him to come to the King of Comedy," which is how Paar often referred to himself, and the dog came to me! That's how I became the King of Comedy.

I got home at about two in the morning and crawled into bed beside my wife, Florence, who was half asleep. She muttered, "How did the dog do all those things?" and I said, "I don't know." She sort of went back to sleep and then she half woke up again and said, "Maybe the man explained everything to the dog before the show."

○●○○●○

Practical

jokes

○●○●○

Alfred Lunt arranged to have the stage manager ring the onstage telephone unexpectedly during a scene.

"Why don't you see who that is?" a smirking Lunt said to his wife, Lynn Fontanne.

Fontanne picked up the phone, said hello, listened, and then turned to Lunt.

"It's for you."

———————O———————

I DO NOT approve of practical jokes on-stage, the great Alfred Lunt notwith-standing. Practical jokes backstage are quite another matter.

When a Broadway show first opens, everyone in the company is up for the first few weeks but then, human nature being what it is, everyone tends to get rather complacent and easygoing about things. The actors who were getting to the theater an hour or even two hours before the curtain will now start to walk through the stage door the very last few seconds before half-hour. Somehow this is especially true of musicals.

My Fair Lady was in the Mark Hellinger Theater, which had only two dressing rooms that could be called dressing rooms. They, of course, were given to the stars, Rex Harrison and Julie Andrews. But otherwise all the men were in one big dressing room and all the women in another. The men's dressing room was four flights up from the stage level. As soon as the show settled in for its five-year run, all the guys started a long series of poker and chess games. Relying on hearing their cues through the speaker system in the dressing room, they played their games to the very last moment before jumping into their costumes, running down the stairs, and making their entrances.

A couple of months after the show opened, the album came out. A friend of mine who was in the chorus sneaked the album and a portable record player into the dressing room. When there was still about fifteen minutes left before curtain time, he turned on the phonograph and the overture blasted out. About thirty half-dressed men jumped into the air and went berserk at the same time.

When Ed Begley and I were in *Inherit the Wind* we shared a dressing room. At the beginning Ed did things—little things —to make me think he was homosexual. It made me very uncomfortable. It wasn't until a steady procession of young ladies started visiting him backstage that I realized he was putting me on. In all my years in show business I have never seen anyone quite as active as Ed. It was astonishing. When his voice cracked onstage we always knew what he had been up to. Reggie Rose told me that when they were shooting the movie version of *Twelve Angry Men* Begley broke the record for "nieces" visiting an actor on the set.

Ed and I were in an elevator together at NBC. When he got out on the floor before mine, he shouted as the doors were closing, "I told you not another penny! Now leave me alone!"

○ 343 ○

As I was leaving Sardi's, passing through hordes of out-of-towners who were ogling the stars while waiting for tables, Ed threw both his arms around me and began kissing me repeatedly on my mouth. I was trying to break loose but he wouldn't let go. "Tony, what's the matter with you? You used to love it!"

If, as Freud postulated, cruelty underlies all varieties of humor, then surely the cruelest form of all is the practical joke, which always has an intended butt, an unwitting victim. On occasion the role gets reversed. Such was the case when Zero Mostel and his close friend Stanley Prager, who went to the same psychoanalyst, decided to concoct an elaborate dream which each recounted in lengthy, exquisite detail at his next day's session. As Mostel, whose hour came after Prager's, concluded, the analyst said, "You know, it's really quite extraordinary. This is the third time today I've heard that dream."

(There is a West Coast version of this same story with a completely different cast of characters: instead of two actors it was two writers: Arthur Laurents and Abe Burrows.)

Hugh Troy was the acknowledged master of the practical joke. Leaving a pile of horse manure late one night in the middle of the Piazza San Marco was one of his greatest achievements. Consternation prevailed the next morning throughout Venice, where in its long history no beast larger than a dog has ever set foot. Such were Troy's exploits—he devoted his life to practical jokes—that *The New Yorker* chronicled them in a fascinating profile.

But when the novelist Richard Condon was earning his living as a movie publicist, he devised an elaborate practical joke that I think ranks with the best of Troy.

The long, nationwide tour to promote *Samson and Delilah,* the newest Cecil B. De Mille epic, was coming to an end. Henry Wilcoxon, the film's very distinguished associate producer and De Mille's right-hand man, was exhausted.

"There's just one more appointment

on the schedule," said Condon, who was publicizing the picture for Paramount. "It's with a priest from the Legion of Decency and a woman from the Protestant Women's Council. And then that's it," Condon assured Wilcoxon.

The priest, very much a New York waterfront type, and the well-groomed, rather prim woman wearing a conservative dress, steel-rimmed glasses, and a flowered hat, came to Wilcoxon's hotel suite. The priest did most of the talking.

"Mr. Wilcoxon, we liked the picture very much but there's one change you're going to have to make."

"Change?" said Wilcoxon, stiffening.

"Yes," the priest continued, "that scene when Hedy Lamarr and Victor Mature are walking hand in hand through the fields. You're going to have to superimpose the image of Jesus over it."

"But that scene takes place centuries before Jesus was born."

"I'm sorry, but that's what you're going to have to do."

"Now, look here," said Wilcoxon, bridling, "the picture is finished. We're about to release it. What you're asking for is absolutely impossible."

"Listen, Mr. Wilcoxon, that's what has to be done, otherwise the Legion is going to condemn your picture. Now, are you going to get on the phone with Mr. De Mille or am I?"

The representative of the Protestant Women's Council, who had remained silent until now, excused herself to go to the bathroom.

It was a hot summer's day and while Wilcoxon pondered, and Condon just sat there, the priest reached into his breast pocket for his handkerchief. As he removed it, two condoms fell onto the carpeted floor. Wilcoxon was aghast, but the priest was unfazed.

"Can't be too careful. There's a lot of VD in my parish," he said as he wiped his sweaty brow and leaned over to pick up the condoms.

At that moment the woman reentered the room. Except for her flowered bonnet and eyeglasses, she was naked.

"Okay," she said, "who wants it first?"

For a moment or two Wilcoxon sat there in stunned, incredulous silence. And then he began to laugh. And so did they all.

When the laughter finally stopped, Condon explained that the "priest" was an actor and the woman a prostitute. He had hired them both, written the scenario, and rehearsed them carefully. It was Condon's way of cheering up Wilcoxon and thanking him on behalf of Paramount Pictures for his yeoman's service on behalf of the picture.

A practical joke crafted in Hollywood runs Condon's a close second. The principals involved were a character actor and a writer. There are some who say it was actually two writers: Julie and Phil Epstein, those identical twins I've mentioned previously. The actor, a habitual freeloader, was always borrowing things from his neighbor, the writer. The writer decided to put an end to it, once and for all. He laid an ingenious trap for the actor, who

○ 348 ○

was becoming increasingly anxious about losing his hair.

"What's this?" asked the actor as he picked up a jar marked FORMULA X in the writer's bathroom.

"Oh," the writer replied, "it's supposed to be some kind of miracle cure for balding. A friend of mine's brother developed it. He's a research chemist at the University of Chicago. It's supposed to be a big breakthrough."

"Can I borrow it?"

"Sure," the delighted writer replied.

The trap was sprung.

For the next several weeks, wherever the actor went—Schwab's Drugstore, the market, the gas station, the studio—everyone who was in on it, and there were many, commented on his growing, thickening hair. He was convinced that the formula was working its magic. And then one day the writer knocked on his door and handed him a telegram. "Here, you better read this."

STOP USING FORMULA X, the telegram from the research chemist in Chicago

read. IT CALCIFIES THE TESTICLES. GO TO
SCHWAB'S PHARMACY IMMEDIATELY. HAVE WIRED
THEM THE ANTIDOTE.

The actor, in a panic, rushed over to
Schwab's, where the pharmacist, who
was also in on it, handed the actor a large
bottle.

"You must rub this stuff into your testicles for about fifteen minutes, six times a
day, without fail."

And so every few hours, for the next
several weeks, the actor applied the antidote to his testicles. Whenever he excused
himself to go to the men's room, everyone
knew why he was going. In due course
the writer came clean but the actor, at
first, refused to believe him. After a while
the actor accepted the fact that he was being taught a lesson. He tells the story himself and claims the antidote grew hair on
his testicles.

Before Joe Mankiewicz started shooting *The Quiet American* in Vietnam, he
was about ninety miles outside of Saigon
on what British crews refer to as a "reccy"
—short for reconnaissance—and Ameri-

cans call location scouting. Mankiewicz, who was peering through a viewfinder, and some of his staff, including his cameraman, production designer, production manager, and Mike, were standing in the middle of a two-lane road, surrounded by rice paddies as far as the eye could see. Several Vietnamese peasants, Vietcong at night, no doubt, wearing nothing but loincloths and conically shaped straw hats, were squatting on their haunches just a few meters away staring at the group in bewilderment. Mike found the situation irresistible. He had the interpreter go over to one of the natives and coach him to stand in front of Mankiewicz and speak to him in Vietnamese. Mankiewicz, who had no way of knowing what was being said to him, asked the interpreter for a translation.

"He wants to know if you aren't Joseph L. Mankiewicz, the famous Hollywood writer, director, and producer."

Mankiewicz gave the Vietnamese, who undoubtedly had never even seen a movie, the biggest smile imaginable. Perhaps it was the intense tropical heat, but for a moment or two Mankiewicz was terribly impressed with himself.

"Now, how the hell would someone all the way out here know—" he began to say.

And then he stopped. He realized he had been had.

There's one rather simplistic practical joke that's been done over and over again on movie sets. It has to be one of the oldest gags in movies and yet it almost always works. I know it did on me. I had a scene in which I was supposed to be asleep. The director said, "Action." I waited for "cut." After about five minutes I said to myself, *How much sleep does he need, for God's sake?* I opened my eyes and discovered that I was all alone on the set.

One promising Hollywood career actually ended because of a practical joke. Eddie Bracken, who became a star in two Preston Sturges films—*Hail the Conquering Hero* and *Miracle of Morgan's Creek*—did the best imitation in show business of

Franklin Delano Roosevelt, with the possible exception of Art Carney. Whenever FDR addressed the nation on radio, Adolph Zukor, the president of Paramount Pictures and a Roosevelt worshiper, had everyone on the lot assemble in the studio's commissary to listen. On this particular occasion, during the Second World War, Bracken got a studio sound technician to connect a microphone to the speakers in the vast room where all had gathered. Two minutes before Roosevelt was to speak, Bracken, out of everyone's sight, began:

"My friends, in the past it has been my sad duty to inform you of our heavy losses in the Pacific. Today, it is with a gladdened heart that I am able to report to you that we are beating the living shit out of the Japs. . . ."

They were, it seems to me, an unlikely choice, but Sam Goldwyn hired Charles MacArthur and his longtime collaborator Ben Hecht to write the screenplay of *Wuthering Heights.* The team worked in the study of Goldwyn's home, where they were living as the producer's guests. A condition of their deal was that they would not have to give Goldwyn anything to read until they had completed the first draft. But Hecht and MacArthur knew that every night Goldwyn was sneaking into the study to read that day's pages. What Goldwyn didn't know was that Hecht and MacArthur were leaving dummy pages for him to find and they were purposefully awful. As frustrated as Goldwyn was, he couldn't say anything.

What follows was not a practical joke, but it may just as well have been. Two of the major forces in the British film industry were John and Roy Boulting, who were identical twins. John died not very long ago and was taken to a funeral home, where a mortician did all those things to prepare a body for burial. When he finished working on John, he stepped outside to take a breather just as Roy was entering the mortuary. No one had bothered to tell the undertaker that the deceased had a twin brother. He fainted.

There was actually an actress—I believe she was Austrian—with the bizarre name of Gisella Werbicek Piffle. Donald Ogden Stewart, a screenwriter, called her one day and said, "Hello, Gisella, this is Don."

"Who?"

"Don Stewart."

"I don't believe I know a Don Stewart," she replied.

"This is Gisella Werbicek Piffle, isn't it?"

"Yes."

"But you were my date at the senior prom at Harvard."

"I have never been to a senior prom at Harvard."

"You haven't?"

"No."

"Oh," said Stewart, "I'm terribly sorry. I must have the wrong Gisella Werbicek Piffle."

My dear friend Groucho was certainly not above practical jokes. He in fact delighted in them.

It was open house at Groucho's every

Sunday. When Harry Kurnitz arrived, Groucho welcomed him.

"Harry, you know who's here? Old man May of the May Company. I don't have to tell you how rich he is. And he's proud of it. But he's a little eccentric. He might try to show you some of his money. If he does, please don't embarrass him. Don't make a big thing of it. Humor him. He's a guest in my house." Groucho then told David May that Harry Kurnitz was at the party.

"He's a blacklisted writer, David. He hasn't made a dime in quite a long while. Have you got a $5 bill in your pocket?"

"Yes, I suppose so. Why?"

"Show it to Harry. He hasn't seen any money in a long time."

"Are you kidding?"

"No," Groucho said, "I'm absolutely serious. Do it for me. Show him $5."

Groucho then went back to Kurnitz.

"May's going to do it, Harry. He's going to show you some of his money. I tried but I can't stop him. He's just an eccentric millionaire, so please indulge him. Tell him you like it."

A little while later, with Groucho watching from across his living room, two perfectly sane people came together and one of them pulled a $5 bill out of his pocket and the other stood there admiring it.

Some
funny
people

---

*Arthur Stanton acquired the distribu-
tion rights in America for the Volks-
wagen automobile, and took his lean
and very lanky friend Harry Kurnitz,
the playwright and screenwriter, for
his very first ride in a Beetle.*

"What do you think, Harry?"

*"Art," said Kurnitz as he unfolded
his way out of the first of the sub-com-
pacts, "I've been in roomier women."*

WE ARE ALL familiar with the famous, legendary funny people
of show business. But there are
others, no less funny, who, if they were
known at all to people outside of the business, have since been forgotten. Those are
some of the men and women to whom I'd
like to devote this chapter.

Consider someone like Harry Ruby,
the songwriter. MGM made a movie about
him and his partner, Bert Kalmar, who

wrote such standards as "Three Little Words," and "I Want to Be Loved By You" as well as the songs for most of the Marx Brothers movies. Ruby and Kalmar, two talented and witty men, who were portrayed by Red Skelton and Fred Astaire in the movie *Three Little Words,* which somehow managed to make them seem dull. *Three Little Words'* sole distinction as a movie musical was that its plot enabled the great Astaire to dance exactly once.

Ruby a tall, lanky redhead was described by George S. Kaufman as looking like a dishonest Abe Lincoln. He was an original. He once confided to Saul Chaplin, a fellow songwriter and a dear friend, that when he was in his early twenties and already reasonably well established on Tin Pan Alley, he was frequently depressed and often had thoughts of suicide. Chaplin asked him if he had ever tried.

"No."

"How come?"

"I don't know," said Ruby rather wistfully, "I was out of town so much."

Ruby came up to Chaplin at one of those big Hollywood parties and said with some urgency, "Come with me. I've got to ask you a very important question."

Chaplin followed Ruby as he threaded his way through the densely packed room to a quiet corner.

"Tell me," Ruby said, "do you think now would be a good time for a hit picture?"

Returning to work at MGM after an absence of about six months, Ruby was being brought up-to-date on all that had transpired at the studio during his absence. Ruby asked about Sam Katz, a producer who had his own unit at the studio.

"He's out. They gave him five percent of the profits of all his completed pictures, fifteen percent of the profits on the pictures he had in preparation, plus a million dollars in cash."

"That'll teach the son of a bitch," Ruby said.

Ann Frank, wife of Mel Frank, the writer and director whom I've mentioned previously, was one of those funny people whom virtually no one but people in the business ever knew about. What made her even funnier was her stammer.

Ann, Mel, and his mother, then in her nineties, were having dinner when the old lady excused herself to go to the bathroom. When she didn't return after a reasonable amount of time, Mel and Ann went to the bathroom and knocked on the door. There was no response. They walked in and there was Mel's mother sitting on the toilet, dead.

Stammered Ann, who was never known to resist a wisecrack, "When you've g-g-g-got to g-go you've g-g-got to g-go."

But it wasn't only Ann's wisecracks. She always had funny stories to tell, most often self-mocking, about some crazy experience she'd had. She was once traveling from New York to Los Angeles on a transcontinental train when a fellow passenger winked at her from the door of his compartment, asked her if she'd like a drink, pulled out a bottle, and offered her a swig.

"Look," said Ann stammering, "if you expect to seduce a woman on a transcontinental train, you've got to be a little smoother about it. Invite her into the bar car, sit there and smooth-talk her over a drink or two, buy her dinner, and then ask her to come back to your compartment."

"I know all about that, lady, but I'm getting off in Kansas City."

The Franks didn't have a very happy marriage, but for various reasons, among them California's community property laws, it survived far longer than most in Hollywood. Mel was raiding the fridge late one night when he collapsed, the victim of a major heart attack. The thud of his fall awakened Ann, who rushed into the kitchen, took one look at Mel on the floor in agony, and called the paramedics. As they waited for the ambulance, she asked Mel, who was still prostrate on the floor, if there was anything she could do for him.

"Yes," he moaned, "move out."

Joe Frisco, the vaudeville comic, was another stammerer. He was on the membership committee of the Lambs Club in New York when Clifton Webb, the actor, best remembered as "Mr. Belvedere," was proposed for membership. A homophobe on the committee objected strenuously.

"We don't want him in this club, for Christ's sake! He's a faggot and we already have two faggots in the club."

"Yeah," Frisco responded, "b-but what if one of 'em d-dies?"

Frisco, leaving the Lambs Club after lunch, passed a huge excavation down the block.

"Wha-what are you b-building?" he yelled down to the workmen.

"A subway," they shouted back.

"How l-long is it going to t-t-take?"

"About five years."

"The hell with it. I'll t-take a cab!"

Frisco always refused to work for a penny less than his established, headliner's price, $3000 a week. As a consequence he didn't work for long periods of time. His agent called Frisco at his hotel and said he had a firm offer of $1500 a week. Frisco turned it down.

"Why don't you at least walk over to my office, Joe, so we can discuss it?"

"W-what, and t-take a chance on g-g-getting locked out of my room for non-payment of rent?"

Late one night Frisco was taking a stroll and ran into an old vaudeville buddy who was down on his luck. Frisco took him back to his hotel room, ordered a sumptuous meal for him, and invited his friend to spend the night. The phone rang. It was the manager.

"You have a guest in your room and if he's spending the night, he'll have to register and you'll have to pay the double occupancy rate."

"Ok-kay," Frisco stammered, "but then you're g-going to have to send up another B-Bible."

Harry Kurnitz was a mumbler but he mumbled funny. He referred to Frank Loesser's first wife, Lynne, as "the evil of two Loessers." Loesser, who lived with his wife in Hollywood, had a girlfriend in New York whom Kurnitz dubbed "East Lynne."

Art Buchwald, Peter Stone, and Kurnitz were sitting in Fouquet's on the Champs-Elysées reading the Paris *Herald Tribune*'s report on the Broadway opening of *Bells Are Ringing*. The musical, starring Judy Holliday and their buddy, Sydney Chaplin, was a smash hit, destined to have a long run.

Said Kurnitz to the others, "I do not want to live in a world in which Sydney Chaplin has a steady job."

A Broadway columnist, notorious for running pointless stories, had just come back from a trip abroad. Kurnitz spotted him entering a New York restaurant.

"Look," said Kurnitz to the friends he was dining with, "the return of no point."

Kurnitz and some friends, dining at a restaurant in Paris, were served a bizarre rice dish that all of them found inedible.

"Do you realize," Kurnitz mumbled, "that tonight there are 850,000,000 Chinese who are eating better than we are?"

Before leaving for an extended motion-picture location on the Continent, Kurnitz gave his friend Sue Barton a dog.

When he returned he asked her how the animal was.

"Harry, it's a very peculiar animal. Not only does he shit all over the place, but he eats it."

"Don't you realize, Sue, that I've given you a dog that you'll never have to feed again for the rest of its life?"

When Ernest Borgnine and Ethel Merman married, Kurnitz said, "I want the pick of the litter." Barely a month later the two highly volatile personalities announced that they were divorcing. "That's a long time," Kurnitz commented, "for a bare-knuckle fight."

To me Wilson Mizner was one of the greatest of all American wits, but whenever I mention him now very few people seem to know whom I'm talking about. Alva Johnston wrote an extraordinary series of *New Yorker* profiles about Wilson and his brother Addison, the famous architect. It is, I believe, the longest series of profiles in the history of that magazine, so fascinated did Johnston and his editors become with their subject. There can be no chapter on funny people without at least a few stories about Mizner, who was a prospector for gold in the Yukon, a Hollywood screenwriter, a Broadway playwright, a fight manager, a gambler, and a host of other things. But most of all he was a wit. Anita Loos, his lady for a while, based the Clark Gable character in *San Francisco* on Mizner.

At one marathon table stakes poker session, he and another player kept raising and seeing each other until they both ran out of chips. His opponent thereupon threw his wallet into the pot. Mizner, without hesitating, bent over, removed his shoe, threw it into the pot, and said, "If we're betting leather, I'll see you."

Mizner had the exclusive rights in the United States to a German process for reproducing art masterpieces. The gallery he opened in New York flourished until the stock market crashed in 1929. He got a call from the manager of his gallery.

"There's someone here who's offering $100 for da Vinci's *The Last Supper*. Should I accept it?"

○ 370 ○

"Absolutely not," Mizner responded, "I won't take less than $10 a plate."

Mizner was married for a time to Mary Yerkes, the widow of the multimillionaire Charles T. Yerkes, and they lived together in her Fifth Avenue mansion. Always something of a rogue, Mizner wanted to insure her life without her knowing about it. The insurance company required a sample of her urine and Mizner, never easily daunted, went to a librarian he knew and asked her to accommodate him.

"If you'll do this for me, I'll treat you and your mother to a first-class round-trip all-expenses-paid tour of Europe."

When the lab report came back, it seems the librarian had what the French call the German disease. After a little while had gone by, she called Mizner to ask about her trip to Europe.

"Europe!" Mizner bellowed. "You couldn't pee your way to Hoboken!"

The Jack Lemmon character in Bernard Slade's play and movie *Tribute* is based, in part, on Harvey Orkin, whose reputation as an irreverent wit was limited almost entirely to people in show business, or at least it was in this country. Orkin was a celebrity in England, where, while working in London as an agent, he became the resident American wit on a popular weekly television show. For most of his life, which ended much too soon, Harvey was an agent. He was still living in New York when he wrote to his close friend, role model, and fellow bon vivant S. J. Perelman, who was living in London at the time. *"I will be there soon. We must visit some museums and libraries together if any are open at two in the morning."*

His closest friend, Jerry Davis, our producer on *The Odd Couple*, married Nancy Gimbel (nee May), whom Orkin had never met. On Orkin's next trip to the West Coast he went right from the airport to the newlyweds' home. He was told that the Davises were in the garden. Orkin went outside and saw a Japanese gardener on a ladder stringing multicolored light bulbs through the branches of some trees. Orkin walked right past Jerry and his bride, climbed the ladder, kissed the gardener, and said, "You must be Nancy."

Jerry was in London pitching a new television series when the meeting was interrupted by a secretary who told him that his doctor was calling from New York. He instructed the secretary to say he would call back. The meeting continued, and once again the secretary entered and told Jerry that his doctor, Kronkite by name, was calling again and that it was an emergency. Jerry, of course, knew that it couldn't be anyone but Harvey Orkin, who was using the name of the famed doctor in the classic Smith and Dale vaudeville sketch—"I'm Kronkite," "I'm dubious," "Hello, Dubious."

"Tell him I'll call back."

After a while the secretary interrupted the meeting once more.

"The doctor called to say that you shouldn't put the salve on the hairy parts of your body."

Davis and Orkin were in a crowded elevator together and as Davis was getting off at his floor, Orkin said, just as the doors were closing, "How did you make out on that morals charge?"

The next time they were in a crowded elevator together, as Davis was getting off he thought he would turn the tables on Orkin. "How did you make out on that morals charge?"

"Fine," Orkin replied. "The boy apologized."

Gisella, Orkin's wife, gave birth to a son, and Sybil Christopher, then Mrs. Richard Burton, came to visit her in the hospital. She expressed her desire to become the boy's godmother.

"That's fine with us," Orkin replied, "but you realize that one of the godmother's responsibilities in the Jewish religion is that she has to bite off the foreskin."

After Harvey died of a brain tumor, Gisella found a farewell note he had left for her in one of his drawers. It was a beautiful and touching expression of the great love he felt for his wife and their two children. At its conclusion he wrote, *"With warmest personal regards."*

16

○●○●○

Opera

○●○●○

Contending with all the highly temperamental singers makes life for an opera conductor arduous. Arturo Toscanini left the opera to become the conductor of the New York Philharmonic. He was walking down Fifth Avenue five years later when a fellow conductor, Sir John Barbirolli, ran into him. "How marvelous you look, Maestro."

"Of course," Toscanini responded, "five years without opera!"

WHEN I GOT out of the Army I was entitled to four years of training under the GI Bill of Rights. I decided to put it into my speaking voice. I knew enough about voice to know that the best way to develop it was to study singing, because it's only on the long, sustained tones that the throat muscles get enough of a workout to grow.

I found a teacher, Henry Jacobi, and went to him until he died, thirty-two years later. Not only did he build my voice but he also saved my life—he forced me to quit smoking. I never had any thoughts about becoming a singer. I found out along the way that I could sing—I have a nice, healthy tone but it's not terribly musical. Musicality is something that can't be taught—if beautiful voices are golden, mine is aluminum. It's like charm in acting: it's nothing that a director can ask of an actor. You either have it or you don't.

I went to the opera for the first time because my teacher told me to go to hear the fully developed result of what we were working on, to hear what the human voice could be. Leonard Warren was singing *Falstaff,* Verdi's last masterpiece, with Fritz Reiner conducting. The first time Warren opened his mouth, that enormous, effortless tone simply floated out and filled the huge auditorium. I walked out of the Met that night hooked. I became an opera nut.

A friend of mine, Harold Greenwald, a

psychologist—the brother of Michael Kidd, the director/choreographer—told me he had a patient, a fifty-eight-year-old homosexual, who had never had intercourse with a woman. He wanted to change and with Harold's help he did. At fifty-eight he had intercourse with a woman for the first time in his life. And he went bananas! That's all he did from morning to night. He never got out of bed. He said to Harold, "Do you mean I could've been doing this all my life?" That's exactly the way I felt when I first went to the opera. "This has always been here? All I had to do was walk in off the street?"

I used to pass the Met almost every day when it was still on Thirty-ninth Street and Broadway. I did a nightly radio show at WOR, which was just across the street. But I never went in. Opera, I thought, was not for me. It had never occurred to me what opera was: that it's a supertheater, theater raised that much higher. And when the acting is good, as it sometimes is, then it's better than good—

it's great. We have no acting to compare to operatic acting when it's great. Naturalism, the style that prevails in the theater, is, after all, a relatively recent development in the history of acting. In fact, I think Jon Vickers, the Canadian tenor, is the greatest living actor. I took Sanford Meisner to see him just so he'd know what I was talking about. Vickers is so big —so overflowing with life—he's like a creature from the Sistine Chapel come to life. You very seldom see theatrical acting on this level. Olivier, occasionally, in Shakespeare.

As I became known, the woman who put on those intermission broadcasts at the Met invited me on the show and I became known as an opera maven. But I'm hardly an expert. I have a fan's knowledge.

Some cultivated people despise opera. They think it's all organ-grinder music. I went to a Budapest String Quartet all-Beethoven recital at the Wilshire Ebell Theatre in Hollywood and ran into Mike Gordon, who directed me in *Pillow Talk.*

"Oh, Tony," he greeted me, "I see you like *good* music too."

The trouble with opera stories is that the surprisingly few good ones have almost all been told.

My favorite opera is Verdi's *Otello,* a really stupendous work. Only a towering genius at the height of his creative powers would have the courage to attempt to enhance a great work like Shakespeare's *Othello.* There are many who believe the opera is actually better than the play. Even the most ardent Wagnerians will concede that *Otello* is the Everest of operas. One of the great Otellos of our time —and I have never seen a bad Otello— was Mario Del Monaco. He was doing it in Philadelphia—his days at the Met were over—and I took the train down to see him. The Moor's entrance is one of the greatest in all of opera: *"Esultate!"* Exult, we have beaten the Turks! Del Monaco, who had a magnificent physique, entered stripped to the waist. But his Negro makeup ended at his neck. That was, without doubt, the single biggest laugh I have ever heard in a theater.

Why, you ask, would Del Monaco have done anything like that? Because he was an Italian tenor and they're famous for being crazy.

If a tenor's high C has, as they say, a "speck of dust on it," nothing else matters. If he doesn't make his high C—if it wobbles just a bit—a tenor is suicidal. The fact that he may have made a phrase in the next act that no one else could emulate means nothing. Tenors are like a man on a tightrope. They're judged by that one note in the entire opera. They judge themselves by that one note. It's a miserable life. It can drive them crazy. They are said to abstain from making love because they think sex brings down a man's voice. I said this on the Dick Cavett show and I got a charming letter from Richard Tucker, who said, "I wish you would interview my wife." But Tucker, of course, was not an Italian tenor—he was Jewish —and he didn't have a high C anyway. Neither did Caruso, for that matter, except on records. He wouldn't chance it in a performance. When Caruso first auditioned for Puccini for *La Bohème* he said, "Maestro, I don't have the high C," and Puccini said, "The way you sing, it doesn't matter."

On tour with the Met, Ezio Flagello was seated on a train between the wives of two famous tenors. "How long has it been for you?" "Three months." "How long for you?" "Four months." And Flagello, a basso, said, "If I can be of service to either of you ladies . . ."

There was a famous tenor at the Met who actually did go bonkers. He had a gorgeous voice which he never really learned to use properly. In rehearsals he took to kissing his hand and placing it on his throat whenever he hit a good note. And then he began doing it in performances.

There is no one who sings better than Luciano Pavarotti. He sings with such beautiful phrasing—he has musical genius. He needs to hear something only once or twice and then he'll begin to phrase it in such a glorious way that it would make a composer rise from his grave and bring tears to his eyes.

I was standing backstage during a Pavarotti performance and one of the assistant maestros said to me, "Listen to that. No other singer on earth can do what he just did with that phrase. He can round it out like a violinist and diminuendo it and then go on to the next phrase before he takes the breath, then take a little catch breath that you don't hear so it's all one phrase. He's so incredibly musical and yet he hates himself tonight—the C was only so-so." Pavarotti doesn't transpose his music down as most tenors do. He goes for a high C wherever it is.

Another great tenor of our time was Franco Corelli, who quit, I believe, at the age of fifty-two. He hasn't been replaced. I saw him over and over again in *Turandot*. In the opera's last act his character takes the veil from the Princess's face, an act symbolic of taking her virginity and of opening her eyes to truth as well. It's the loss of innocence. Corelli obviously didn't like this particular soprano who was playing the Princess—I've even forgotten her name—so when he pulled the veil from her face, instead of dropping it onstage, he held on to it, blew his nose in it, and then slowly folded it—once, twice—four times in all—until it was a tiny little packet. And then he threw it away. It was like a Danny Kaye routine.

For years Lorenzo Alvary was a basso with the Met. In his opinion Ezio Pinza, the Italian basso, was the greatest voice of the past hundred years. "The difference between my voice and Pinza's," Alvary has said, "is like the difference between New York and Kalamazoo." When the Met was appearing in Sacramento, California, Bidu Sayão and Pinza were doing Massenet's *Manon.* At the very last minute Alvary replaced Pinza, who was scheduled but couldn't appear as the Count. Alvary wore Pinza's wig and his costume. The next day the papers all said that Pinza was in excellent voice and a great success in the role. At the next performance, when it was made clear to the audience and the critics that it would be Alvary and not Pinza appearing as the Count, they never even mentioned him. Alvary was simply ignored.

Alvary, while a young singing student in Milan, earned money as a claqueur at La Scala. He and about fifteen others were given a seat at each performance by a Mr. Forsatti, who told them for whom and when and for how long they had to clap. Forsatti, of course, was paid by the artists accordingly. One night during *Rigoletto* they were supposed to applaud for a young American soprano, but Alvary's musicality wouldn't permit him to do it. The next day Forsatti said, "Hey, young man, why didn't you applaud yesterday for that soprano?"

"You can kill me, you can do anything you want, but my conscience just wouldn't permit me to do it. I'm sorry."

"All right, if you're going to be like that, then I can no longer give you a seat."

The next day Alvary ran into Forsatti, who told him he was a very intelligent young man.

○ 386 ○

"Why?" Alvary asked.

"Because," Forsatti replied, "she didn't pay me."

At my New York gym one day I overheard the manager pitching a prospective member.

"We get a lot of celebrities here . . . Tony Randall, Sherrill Milnes . . ."

"Who?"

"Sherrill Milnes—the opera star."

"Daytime or nighttime?"

I am normally the mildest of men, but one evening at the Met during a Joan Sutherland performance of *Lucia di Lammermoor* I was sitting behind a man who drove me mad. He was conducting throughout the performance and it was very distracting. Finally I reached out and grabbed him so hard that I almost broke his shoulders. He, too, is an opera buff, whom I frequently see at the Met. Whenever I catch his eye, he cringes.

It's a sad fact that operas are generally put on with very little rehearsal. The star often arrives just in time for the performance. The great stars are on an international circuit—New York, London, Rio de Janeiro, Milan, San Francisco—and they're flying to and from opera houses all the time.

In *Aida* when all the slaves are brought in, she's supposed to recognize her father among them. My friend Birgit Nilsson told me that when that moment came during a performance of *Aida* at one of the major opera houses, she had no idea which one of the throng of over one hundred was her father. She thought it must be the tallest and most kingly and she went to him. Actually, it was Aldo Protti, who was the shortest.

To Rudolf Bing goes the honor of having racially integrated the Met. Soon after Leontyne Price's historic debut in *Il Trovatore,* Martina Arroyo joined the Met as the Heavenly Voice in *Don Carlo.* One day the stage doorman greeted Arroyo as "Miss Price."

"No, dearie," Arroyo responded, "I'm the other one."

Nowhere is Murphy's Law more in evidence than at the opera.

How many times has Siegfried's anvil broken before the tenor has had a chance to cleave it with his sword, or has Brünnhilde put on her horned helmet backward, or has the swan boat come and gone without Lohengrin? And, of course, very often the animals onstage misbehave during performances. Sir Thomas Beecham remarked when a horse did it to him during a performance at Covent Garden, "My God, a critic."

Tosca ends with the suicide of Tosca. She runs to the ramparts of the Castel Sant' Angelo on the banks of the Tiber, where every American tourist has been, she screams, "Scarpia, we meet before God!" and leaps off the parapet. Of course she lands on a pile of mattresses. Many are the stories of the huge soprano who has bounced back into the audience's view.

I actually saw Montserrat Caballé stand on the parapet, shout out the final line—"Scarpia, we meet before God!"— make as if to jump, and then calmly walk offstage.

There's one story that has come back to me in many, many forms, but this is the way it really happened: I was at a dinner party at Zinka Milanov's home and among the guests were Joan Sutherland, who sings in the most beautiful, liquid Italian possible but speaks with a very harsh Australian accent. Over the hubbub of the party we suddenly heard Milanov, the Yugoslavian soprano, say, in her booming voice, "I don't like *Elektra,*"—the Richard Strauss opera—"I don't care who knows it. Too wiolent." And Sutherland responded with a gloss of *Il Trovatore:* "Wrawng byebeez on the fahyre—that's more your stahle—ay, Zink?"

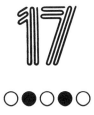

○●○●○

The

end

○●○●○

---○---

"Show me a man who has never thought about his own epitaph and I'll show you someone who has never thought about his own epitaph."

Anonymous

---○---

Who among us has not, from time to time, thought about his or her own epitaph or, for that matter, the epitaphs of others?

Let's start with the apocryphal:

I NEVER THOUGHT I'D LIVE TO SEE THE DAY

SAMUEL GOLDWYN

Then there's W. C. Fields. Even though he was a native, he, like most people in the business, didn't much care for the City of Brotherly Love.

Leonard Bernstein is a brilliant but incessant talker. Almost the only way of having a conversation with him is to interrupt. But he hates to be interrupted.

At the beginning of his film career, before he went on to win four Academy Awards for writing and directing, Joe Mankiewicz was mostly known in Hollywood as Herman's kid brother. Joe, in fact, was convinced for a time that his epitaph would read:

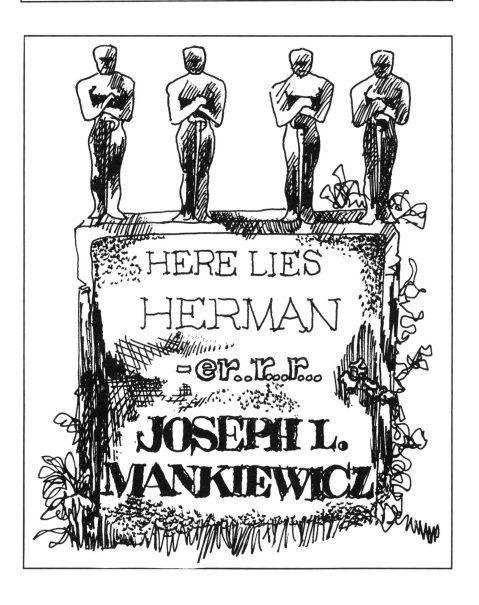

HERE LIES
er...r...r..r
Oh you know-
What's his
name...
er...
Oh, God...
I'll think of it...
The producer...
Music Man...
Death of a Salesman...

HERE LIES LUCIANO PAVAROTTI

THE FAT LADY SANG

HERE
LIES

JEROME
ROBBINS

Conceived by
Lena & Harry
Rabinowitz

Sacha Guitry and Yvonne Printemps were the Lunt and Fontanne of the French theater. Printemps was not only beautiful but exuded passion on- and offstage. Guitry suggested the following for her epitaph:

HERE LIES
Yvonne
Printemps
COLD
FOR THE FIRST TIME

And after they were divorced, Printemps suggested the following for Guitry's epitaph:

We had our differences, of course, but thanks to our editor.